Coachbear 30
The Life and Times of Coach Larry Geigle

COACHBEAR

The Life and Times of Coach Larry Geigle

by **LARRY GEIGLE**

Inkwater Press®
inkwater.com

Publisher: Inkwater Press | www.inkwaterpress.com

Paperback
ISBN-13 978-1-62901-544-6 | ISBN-10 1-62901-544-x

1 3 5 7 9 10 8 6 4 2

CONTENTS

CHAPTER THREE

JUNIOR HIGH SCHOOL

CHAPTER FOUR

MY FATHER AND BROTHERS

CHAPTER FIVE

HIGH SCHOOL

PROLOGUE

Larry Geigle, my husband of fifteen years, hobbles over to the table that I have reserved for us in this little coffee shop in McMinnville, Oregon. He is a striking man in his late sixties; his oversized cane makes *clomp-clomp-clomp* noises on the hardwood floor. He has a full head of stark-white hair and looks healthy—with a tanned, outdoorsy complexion, and twinkling brown eyes. The only thing that ages him is his gait, and the cane. As he walks toward me, he lists to starboard—although he maintains a painless, almost serene expression. In all the years I've known him, he hasn't changed much.

"Coachbear 30" (30 is his high school football jersey number) is on a mission: He wants to write a book about his life for his children and grandchildren, so they might know him a little better. As we sit in the coffee shop, Larry begins to tell his story and what he thinks the book should be about.

He wants his readers to understand that this book is about a young man getting knocked down and getting back up again. Larry stops and looks out the window, then continues to explain his thoughts on the book. He says the book is also about a young man who falls in love with the game of football because his coach believed in him. Then he gets hurt serving his country during the Viet Nam War, and ends up losing his childhood sweetheart while having to deal with the effects of PTSD. He fights on, daring to fulfill his dream of being the first in his family to graduate from college and play college football. After trying out and making the team, and overcoming injury and road blocks, he finally plays his first game, setting school records. He is nagged by injury and sickness, and once again, falls short of the recognition he worked so hard to achieve.

After college, he becomes a teacher and coach, helping his students and players find their way. Even though Larry finds comfort in his work, PTSD causes him to stumble and fall once again. His first marriage ends. His life becomes inconsistent. His relationship with his kids suffers. He has no idea why he feels the way he does, but he keeps trying to understand what his fear, mistrust, and anxiety are all about.

After deciding to leave teaching and coaching, he realizes that was a mistake. He again fights his way back, and now finds himself working as an assistant principal. After a few years, even though Larry is well-liked by students, the new principal doesn't agree with Larry's conservative approach. Larry resigns as assistant principal and decides to go back to the classroom as a teacher and coach. He has begun to realize how much the accident in Viet Nam has contributed to a lifetime of pain and anxiety.

In 2003, Larry decided to talk to the US Department of Veterans Affairs regarding issues he felt were affecting his life. Though he had lived with PTSD for over thirty years, the VA denied his claim. For the next three years, Larry and I kept trying to get him help, and after countless attempts and numerous frustrating hospital visits, Larry was finally awarded disability for his PTSD. Even though he has lived with PTSD since 1970, the VA still has not compensated him for all the years before compensation was granted.

Like most of us, he is now doing as he's always done: the best that he can. Even though he is still suffering from PTSD, he hopes that by reading this book you will see that he has been able to have some great moments along the way.

I doubt that anyone wakes up in the morning and says to himself, "Today is going to be an awful day!" Larry is still full of hopes and dreams, and he continues to look for happiness. He's sure he is going to win Publishers Clearing House someday—so he's having fun keeping a positive outlook as much as he can. He's a good man who loves God, life, his children, grandchildren, stepchildren, friends, wife, and Linfield football—not necessarily in that order! He tries to attend as many of his grandkids' sporting events and milestones as he can, and he hopes his children and grandchildren will get to know their grandfather a little better after reading his story.

His example of not giving up is a lesson for all of us. He would like his readers—especially his children and grandchildren—to remember that no matter how hard you get knocked down, you get back up, give them hell, and always do the right thing.

Paula Geigle
March 2018

CHAPTER ONE

CHAPTER ONE
EARLY YEARS

I<small>N</small> 1954, <small>WHEN</small> I <small>WAS</small> 5 <small>YEARS OLD</small>, I <small>CAN RE</small>-member looking down a steep hill in front of our house in Oakland, California. The kids in the neighborhood were having great fun riding down this monster hill, on two roller skates attached to the bottom of a two-by-four. Even though you wore out the seat of your blue jeans on the cement road, you could expect a thrilling ride. The biggest thrill came at the bottom of the hill, because that's where the road ended. Somehow, you had to stop before getting hit by a car passing through the intersection, or before you hit the curb at the end of the street and launched yourself into outer-space. We would stick our feet out, using the heels of our tennis shoes to avoid danger. Somehow, we stopped ourselves, or crashed . . . or did whatever else it took to stop.

Mom, Dad, brothers Mike, Steve and I lived in a small rental home. We had moved to Oakland from Portland, Oregon, after my father had received a promotion. He was now the manager of the shoe department of a Nordstrom in downtown Oakland. We weren't rich, or had fancy toys, so we three boys came up with a lot of ways to have fun using our imaginations. We were good kids, but full of energy, and we always found new ways to have fun without killing ourselves—although sometimes we got banged up a little. Mike was the oldest, at eight years old. Steve was six, and I was the youngest, at five.

The Garage Hole

ONE SUMMER DAY, WHILE MY FATHER WAS AT WORK, the three of us were hanging out in the garage. We decided it would be great to build a fort. We dug out the floor of the garage and covered the hole with a big piece of plywood. We worked all day. It wasn't easy; all the dirt had to be piled outside in the yard, so it took a huge effort. We were determined to have the fort, thinking it would make an excellent hideout. We talked about putting some household items in it to make it comfortable—maybe a table and some chairs, along with a nice candle for light. We finally got the hole dug, and were pretty tired, to say the least. Then we found some old pieces of plywood and covered the hole. You couldn't even tell it was there.

When my father came home from work that night no one had warned him about our new fort. He drove his car into the garage and . . . you guessed it. He drove right into the hole. When we heard the crash, we all ran out to the garage. There was Dad, sitting in the car, surrounded by a big cloud of dust, with the funniest expression on his face. We took one look and ran for it! I think Dad had to crawl out the back window to get out of the car.

One thing I loved about my dad was that he loved his children. I don't remember him physically punishing us or even yelling at us.

I do remember him making us fill in the hole after the tow truck came and pulled our old '53 DeSoto out. Dad asked how the hole got in the garage floor. We told him we were building a secret hideout and forgot to tell him. After that we were banned from digging any more holes on the property.

The DeSoto Gets a New Look

ONE AFTERNOON, I WAS OUT IN THE GARAGE MESSING around. I saw some paint cans and decided to look them over and see what kind of paint we had. I opened one of the cans and there I saw a beautiful red color. Being five years old I didn't know much about paint, but I did imagine the fun you could have with it. I grabbed a brush from the workbench and dabbed a little red paint on a piece of wood, then stood back and admired how wonderful it looked. I happened to turn at that moment and saw the old blue '53 DeSoto sitting there looking all worn-out and drab. I thought I'd put a little paint on one of the rust spots to help it look better. Sure enough, it spruced it right up. For some reason I just kept painting, and when I was done I had painted both sides of the car as high as I could reach. I thought it looked much better and went into the house to bring out my mother to show her what a wonderful thing I had done. Our blue car was now a beautiful red!

When my mother saw the car, she couldn't believe what I had done. She called for Dad, and when he saw what I had done, he immediately grabbed a can of paint thinner, and for the next few hours, cleaned the paint off the car the best he could. I could only say that I was just trying to help out and make the car look better. I couldn't understand what all the fuss was about.

Dad Just Needed More Gas

IT SEEMED EVERY DAY MY FATHER COMPLAINED about not having enough gas in the '53 DeSoto. One day it was parked out on the driveway, and I was playing in the gravel just behind it with my toy trucks. I loved playing in the dirt, building my future dream house and the roads that led to different garages dug out for all my toy vehicles.

While I was playing, I recalled how my dad was always concerned about not having enough gas for his car. I thought to myself, *If I fill up Dad's gas tank with rocks, he won't need so much gas*. I reached down and grabbed a handful of gravel, opening the fuel door and pouring the gravel down the opening. I thought this was a brilliant idea, and wondered why people didn't use this method more often. When I was done dumping all the rocks in the tank, I went back to playing, and forgot about what I had done. Later that day, Dad took off in the car, and I thought to myself, *He will be so proud that I helped him with the gas problem*.

It wasn't too long before the phone rang. It was Dad—he told my mother that he was on the side of the road, and the car wouldn't run. Dad said he was having the car towed to an auto repair shop. After a lengthy investigation by the repair shop, it appeared the gas tank was filled with rocks.

I heard my mother on the phone, and rushed over with a smile on my face, excitely telling her that I had put the rocks in Dad's gas tank to help with his gas problem. My mother just stared at me in amazement, as if she couldn't believe what she had just heard. Then she put the phone to her ear and explained to Dad, who was still on the phone, what I had done. It sounded like there was some loud screaming on the other end, so my smile left and tears came to my eyes. I guess I hadn't helped Dad at all. By the time he got back home, he had calmed down, remembering that I was only five! As time passed, the rocks in the gas tank became a funny story that Dad told over and over. Like I said, he was a great dad!

How Does That Toilet Work, Anyway?

ONE MORNING, I WAS IN THE HOUSE AND HAD TO GO "number one." I headed to the bathroom, and when I was done, I started to wonder how the toilet worked. Where did all that "number one" and "number two" go? I couldn't believe that just by me pushing the handle, the water went down the hole, never to be seen again. I was amazed at this phenomenon, so I grabbed some toilet paper and put it in the toilet and flushed it down, trying to understand where it went and what made it disappear.

Then I saw one of my Dad's ties hanging on the door—so I grabbed it and put the end in the toilet. I gave the toilet a flush. As I held on to the end of the tie, it started to tug at me like I had a fish on the other end. After the flush was over, I pushed the handle again and again. It tugged as if to tell me to let go—so I did. The tie disappeared . . . to who-knows-where?

Where did it go? I asked myself. I ran to my Dad's closet and got another tie, and tried it again. Once again the tie vanished. It was like magic—I just couldn't figure it out. After about six or seven ties, all of a sudden the ties wouldn't go down anymore. The toilet started to fill up with water. Then it overflowed onto the bathroom floor. I had created a big problem. I flushed again, and the toilet just kept overflowing. It was time to get help.

I ran to my mother and told her the toilet was overflowing. When she arrived on the scene, she let out a major scream. Water was everywhere, and one of the ties was floating in the toilet. I couldn't understand why the ties didn't continue to disappear, and had no idea where all the water was coming from. My mother reached down and pulled the tie out of the toilet and looked at me. She said, "Larry, what have you done?" She ran and got the toilet plunger and plunged away.

The end of one of the other ties was visible, so my mother reached down and grabbed it, pulling it out. The toilet water started to drain. Somehow she was able to get the rest of the ties out, but it took a long time to clean up the mess. She never told Dad—at least not for a long time.

I had survived another day as a five-year-old, and learned a little about how to plug a toilet.

Buried Alive

THIS NEXT STORY IS NOT MY FAVORITE, BUT IT NEEDS to be told. Down at the end of the monster hill was a large lot with an old house on it that hadn't been lived in for quite some time. We all know what these abandoned houses look like. My brother Mike and I, along with some other boys, were down at the abandoned house, digging a hole in the front yard. I don't really remember why we were digging the hole. It was something to do for entertainment, I guess.

Mike came up with the idea of putting me in the hole and burying me up to my neck in dirt. He was going to go home and try to convince my mother that my head was on the ground and the rest of my body had disappeared. I didn't mind it so much until I realized I couldn't move my arms and was completely helpless. I started yelling at them to let me out. Mike laughed; he was having a great time seeing how scared I was. Suddenly I saw a huge bug crawling on the ground, heading for my face. I started screaming like a crazy person. From eye-level, the attacker appeared to be a giant alien, the likes of which I had never seen. I knew he was going to bite me or sting me—it just didn't look good from where I was.

I kept screaming at them to stop that bug and get me out. Just then, a policeman in a patrol car drove by and heard me screaming. He stopped and saw what was going on. Mike reached down and brushed the bug away as the officer came closer, and the officer told him to get me out of the hole. The officer could see I was really scared. When I was finally out, he told Mike to fill in the hole. He asked where we lived. As he walked us up to the house, I had a hard time holding back my tears. The officer told my mother what Mike had been up to and headed on his way. I spent the rest of the day close to my mother. Being buried up to my neck had not been a good childhood experience and I never forgot it.

Two Hundred Cars Stranded at Donner Pass

WE ONLY LIVED IN OAKLAND, CALIFORNIA FOR A year, when my father was transferred back to Portland, Oregon. He was promoted to manage the second-floor shoe department at the downtown Portland Nordstrom. We packed up all our belongings, and when the movers came we watched them load the moving truck and then pull away with all the boxes and furniture. When they were gone, we all jumped in the '53 DeSoto and started our trip back north—to the St. Johns area in Portland, where we would live with our Grandma Geigle until we got settled.

As we headed through the mountains a few hours later, we entered Donner Pass in the Sierra Nevada mountain range of California. Dad hadn't expected to be caught in a full-out blizzard. It started snowing so hard it became a complete white-out. The wind was blowing, making it hard to see the road. All we could do was follow the tail lights in front of us as they led the way.

As we inched along, we could tell everyone was having trouble keeping their cars on the road. It was pretty frightening, to say the least. Suddenly, the car in front of us slid off the road and into a ditch and got stuck. Just a few moments later, our car slid into the ditch also. We couldn't move; we were stuck with two hundred other cars in in a serious blizzard. As we sat there with the snow coming down, our pet parakeet, Ricky, was singing away, having a great time. We sat there for a couple of minutes, and then there was a knock on the window. When my Dad rolled down the window, a police officer smiled and asked if everyone was okay. He then told us no one would be going anywhere until the next day. He told my dad to gather our things and follow him to a bus that was waiting to take us to a hotel up the road.

We grabbed a few things, and realized we would have to leave Ricky in the car overnight. My parents didn't say anything, but I'm sure they thought Ricky wouldn't make it through the night. My mother covered his cage with a blanket, hoping it would keep him warm. We left the car and walked to the bus. The wind blew and the snow piled up in major drifts against the other cars that had slid off the road. When we stepped on the bus, it felt good to get warm and be with other people. Even though it was a serious situation, you could tell everyone was watching out for each other.

When we arrived at the hotel, the snow was really coming down, and I was glad we weren't in the DeSoto. Once inside the hotel, it was like a whole new world. I realized we were safe from the bad storm outside, and that everything was going to be okay. My dad got us our room, and we headed for the restaurant inside the hotel to have a nice hot meal. It was warm and cozy, and now that we were all safe, it was turning out to be a fun adventure.

The next morning, the storm had passed and the sun was shining. I looked through the hotel window to see outside. There were huge mounds of snow piled up against the building along with all the cars in the parking lot. The trees looked beautiful with their limbs full of snow and the sunlight dancing off their new wardrobe.

You could hear the snow plows in the distance, trying to clear the roads. People were talking, digging out their cars, and trying to head on down the road—determined to complete their journey. My dad picked up a newspaper, and there we were on the front page. It read, "Two hundred cars stranded in Donner Pass overnight from huge blizzard."

We got dressed and were in good spirits as we headed downstairs for a nice breakfast. Of course, I had my favorite: French toast! We then went outside and boarded the bus that would take us back to our car. When we arrived, we were all expecting the worst, as my dad opened the door to the DeSoto. To our surprise, Ricky greeted us with his chirping and singing. I'm sure he was happy to see us. We stood and watched as the DeSoto was pulled from the ditch. The roads were now open, so we piled in, and once again headed north to Portland. It was the adventure of a lifetime.

Grandma Geigle's
(1955)

WHEN WE ARRIVED AT GRANDMA GEIGLE'S HOUSE we were all pretty tired. Grandma Geigle was a great cook and owned a little diner in St. Johns, so she was always feeding us boys. She had a large house with an apartment upstairs. We were going to have the whole downstairs to ourselves. All three of us boys would be staying in the same bedroom. Steve and I had a bunk bed and Mike slept on a queen bed against the wall. We found out very quickly that you could jump from the top bunk to the lower bed that was against the wall, just for fun. You just had to be careful you didn't bounce yourself headfirst into the wall.

The house had a large basement with a cement floor that on rainy days was a fine place for us to roller skate. There was a large living room with bookshelves and a red brick fireplace. It was going to be a great place to stay until we found a new house. You could tell my parents were happy to be back in St. Johns, where they had first met.

Sleepwalking to Boone, Iowa

THAT SUMMER AFTER ARRIVING AT MY GRANDMA Geigle's house, my mother decided to visit her mother and sister in Iowa. Since I now was six years old, I would be traveling with my mother by train from Portland, back to Iowa. It was the first train I had ever been on, and I was excited. My brothers were going to stay home on this trip, because they were older and easier to take care of.

When we got on the train, I was amazed at the size of this big machine, and all the excitement around its departure. My mother checked our luggage, and we had some extra time to walk around the huge train depot. The ceilings were really high, and every once in a while you would hear the announcer announce the departure of trains over the loudspeaker. I can remember it echoing throughout the station: "CAN I HAVE YOUR ATTENTION PLEASE: NOW BOARDING THROUGH GATE NUMBER THREE, FOR SPOKANE, BOSIE, AND SALT LAKE CITY. ALL ABOARD, PLEASE."

As we kept walking, we stopped in the little shops displaying souvenirs, candy, and soda, along with other small items to help make traveling a little more enjoyable. My mother bought me a couple of Baby Ruth candy bars and some jawbreakers for our trip. Then over the loudspeaker we heard our train announced—so we went to our gate and then outside to board. There was a long, covered, cement boarding area that the train had to pull up to. As we walked on the loading platform, I noticed big clouds of white steam pouring out from under the train. When we boarded the train, a conductor—dressed in his official uniform and a funny little hat—showed us to our seats.

I sat down by the window, looking out at the depot and all the people outside. A short time later, the conductor stepped off the train and yelled, "ALL ABOARD." Then he stepped back on. I heard the loud train whistle signal our departure and we were on our way.

Just after we left the train depot, we went over the Willamette River and right through St. Johns; just a few blocks from Grandma Geigle's house. A short time later, we crossed over the mighty Columbia River into the state of Washington. As we headed east up the Columbia Gorge toward Spokane I looked at the train's high-backed seats and the weather-worn shades that you could pull down over the windows to shut out the daylight. I took it all in; the sounds of the train moving along with the gentle swaying of the compartments, and every now and then the mighty train whistle giving the countryside a blast, to clear the track. As we traveled through the Gorge and along the Columbia, I could see the beautiful landscape of green fir trees on the other side in Oregon, and the wonderful gray rock formations that had been carved from years of wind and rain. When the conductor came by, he asked for our tickets, gave me a smile, and was on his way. We traveled all day and then settled down in our seats to try and get some sleep.

During the night the conductor woke my mother and delivered me back to my seat. I had been sleepwalking and he found me in the next train car, headed to the other end of the train. It wasn't the first time I had walked in my sleep. My parents had to keep a pretty good eye on me at night. One time, I had gotten up, gone to the living room, kissed the kitty-cat on the forehead, and walked out the front door. They found me walking down the driveway, and my father grabbed me and took me back to bed.

When I was put back in my seat on the train, I slept the rest of the night. When we awoke the next day, we were far from home. I felt pretty special being with my mother while Mike and Steve were back home. It was so nice, having her all to myself. My mother told me we were going to the dining car to have breakfast, and that I should show good manners, and say please and thank you. The dining car was filled with people having breakfast, starting their day with quiet conversation. I had one of my specials: oatmeal, toast, and a glass of orange juice. Looking out the window, I saw that the landscape had changed from mountains to flat farmland, with tall golden grass as far as could you see. I spent all day looking out the window.

The next morning, we pulled into the train station in Boone, Iowa. As we got off the train, Aunt Jo and Homer were there to greet us. Aunt Jo was my mother's oldest sister. My mother hadn't seen her sister in years, and it was quite a welcome. It was the first time they had met me, so there were a lot of hugs and handshakes. Then we all jumped in the car and headed to Aunt Jo's home. When we arrived, we took our suitcases inside, and after a few minutes of conversation, I went outside to look around.

I noticed that Aunt Jo's boys were throwing rocks on the side of the house. I went over and said hello and watched what they were up to. They were trying to hit an object high up in a large tree that stood in their yard. I thought I would join in and impress them. So I picked up a rock and let it fly. Even though I was only six years old, I was already a strong little boy. The rock was a bad idea. It flew out of my hand, high in the air and right through my Aunt Jo's bathroom window, shattering the glass. Aunt Jo and my mother came darting out of the house and asked what was going on. I hadn't been there twenty minutes and I was already was in big trouble. When they learned that I had thrown the rock through the window my mother apologized to her sister. My Aunt Jo played it down, like it was not that big of a problem. I couldn't believe how far I threw that rock. Aunt Jo's house was a big two-story house, and that bathroom window was way up there. I guess I was stronger than I thought!

The rest of the trip went pretty well, except I knocked my milk glass over at the dinner table. That seemed to happen to me a lot, and it became one of my trademarks. My Dad would always give me the look when I spilled my milk. It was as though he wanted to get mad, but couldn't, because he loved me so much. We stayed at Aunt Jo's for the whole week, and before you knew it, we were on the train on our way back home. Once again, I gazed out the window, really enjoying seeing the countryside pass by; but I was happy when we pulled into Portland, and glad to be home. My brothers and Dad were there to meet us. We were all glad to see each other, and soon I was home in my grandma's house, thinking about the trip. When I went outside, all my friends came up to me and told me they were glad I was home.

Chapter Two

GRADE SCHOOL

Problem at Lombard Street
(1955)

THAT FALL, AFTER GOING TO IOWA, I STARTED attending St. Johns Elementary. I was now in the first grade. Even though I was just a little guy, I had to walk a good mile to school, and then home at the end of the day. I developed a serious problem when I walked home every day, and had to cross busy Lombard Street. There was no light or crosswalk, like there is today. I just stood there for the longest time, waiting for a break in the traffic. The problem got even worse when I realized while standing at that street corner that I had to use the restroom—I mean, really bad! I tried to hold it by jumping up and down, but I was always too late. I would start wetting my pants, and felt really bad about it by the time I got home.

My mother couldn't believe it. She told me every day not to wet my pants, but I couldn't help it. I always wondered if people driving by understood the problem I was having, and whether they could see my pants, all wet, as I stood there on the corner. I finally figured out that I needed to go to the restroom right after school, so that by the time I got to Lombard Street I would be okay. I was glad the pee problem had been solved.

Birthday Bird

BEFORE I TELL THIS NEXT STORY, I WANT PEOPLE WHO might read this to know... I don't hurt animals. And even though I was a rough little boy and only six years old, I still think about this now! What if I had hurt that little bird?

One day in early September, I was walking home from school. It was my birthday. I was excited because I believed my dad was bringing home a new baseball glove. That particular day, I was walking home with my new friend, Buzz. Buzz lived on the other side of Lombard Street from Grandma Geigle's house, and a few houses up a side road. He had red hair, plenty of freckles, and stood about my height. We were both full of mischief, and had met while shooting marbles before school.

As we walked home that day, we came to Lombard Street and I happened to hear a bird making a bunch of noise up in a large maple tree, at the corner where I was supposed to cross. I told Buzz I could nail that bird with a rock, and he just laughed as he turned the corner and started down the other side of Lombard toward his house. I picked up the rock and let it fly—once again, a bad idea. Just as I threw the rock, a car pulled up to the street corner, and when the rock came down, there was a loud crash as the windshield broke into hundreds of pieces. Glass was all over the street. The bird flew off; I never came close to hitting it.

Buzz took off running, and so did I. He went for his house and I went for mine. When I got home I ran for the back door and went down into the basement, hiding behind the furnace. I could tell few minutes later there was someone at the front door, talking to my mother. I knew this time that I was in big trouble. I had made a bad decision throwing that rock, and when my dad got home that evening I was going to get killed.

I didn't move. A few hours later the basement door opened. I knew my dad was coming down. Before he said a word I started crying. He asked me what happened and I told him. He held my new baseball glove up in his hand. He told me I needed to think about what I had done and that it would be a while before I would get my new baseball glove. He made it clear: no more rock throwing, or else. I never forgot that day and how bad I felt about hitting that windshield. I was getting older, and my dad was letting me know that he expected better choices in the future.

Francois

ONE DAY, MY MOTHER TOLD US BOYS THAT WE WERE getting a new addition to our family. We would stay with Grandma Geigle while Mom and Dad traveled to Seattle to buy a standard French poodle. Our new friend was already named Francois, and came from a long history of champion show dogs. Francois had a brown nose instead of a black one, so they were willing to sell him for a reduced price of $1,000. Back then, that was a lot of money for a pet, so this wasn't just any dog. My parents thought it would be a great pet for us kids, and a fun addition to the family.

When we got Francois, he was just a little guy. I attached quickly to this little, white, fluffy playmate. Mother became his best friend very quickly, because that's where the food came from. I think I was next in line because I played with him a lot. He was smart, and over a short period of time, we had him sitting, laying down, and even saying please for treats. Francois always stayed close to my mother, and at night would crawl underneath my parents' bed and sleep there until morning.

As the years passed and Francois got bigger, he made quite a rumble when coming out from under the bed in the morning. It would wake up the whole house. We taught him to get my mother's slippers and cigarettes, and to let himself out by opening the sliding glass doors to our house on Bowmont Street. Sometimes, my mother and father would sit on the living room couch, and act like they were kissing. Francois would get jealous and climb up between them. He would start smiling, showing his teeth and sneezing.

Francois became a pretty big dog. When we put music on the radio, I would grab his front paws, put them on my shoulders, and dance around the living room with him. Francois turned out to be a wonderful friend, and part of my childhood. When I was in high school, he jumped down from a table on our deck and twisted his insides. He died in my arms on the way to the vet. It was too late when we got there to save him.

He was the best!

Moving to 123rd
(1956)

DAD DECIDED THAT LIVING IN ST. JOHNS WAS NOT A real good place to raise us boys. So we started looking for a house outside of Portland, in the Beaverton area. It was a fast-growing community with very little crime and a good school district. We didn't have a lot of money, but after looking, managed to buy a nice little two-bedroom house on 123rd street. This home was part of the first addition of houses built right after the Second World War. They were small, but built well.

Our new house sat in what is known today as Old Cedar Hills. After moving in, I found that once again, I was sharing a bedroom with my brothers. Most of these houses were built in a hurry, to supply the returning soldiers a place to raise their families. Most of them only had two bedrooms, but large lots with plenty of room for kids to play.

Mike had a single bed next to the window at the end of the room. If Mike got too mad at me, he would just shove me out the window and lock it. I would have to run around to the front door and ring the doorbell until someone let me back in. Steve was on the top bed of a new trundle bed my parents had purchased, and I was on the bottom. During the day, my bed was pushed under Steve's, and this helped make the bedroom a little bigger. My parents' room was down the hall and to the right, and the only bathroom was at the end of the hall. The front door of the house opened up into the living room, which had hardwood floors that came in handy for sliding around if you had your socks on. A red brick fireplace was on the opposite wall from the front door, with one of those big cheap mirrors over a wood mantle. There was also a small dining room off the living room, where many Parcheesi, Monopoly, and card games were played. Oh yeah—I almost forgot the big bowls of popcorn that were consumed!

Then there was a door that led into a very small kitchen with a window that looked out to the backyard. The backyard was big and grassy. It supplied Francois with plenty of room to run and do "number two"—I remember this because I would step in it. In the front yard, we had a nice maple tree that provided shade in the summer for my lemonade stand. The complete house was only nine hundred square feet. Even though this was a small house, it was filled with some great times. After growing older, I would drive by once in a while, unable to believe how small it was. Lastly, it had a long driveway, where we parked the old DeSoto—which I used for my hideout if I was being chased or in trouble.

Doing It the Hard Way

BEFORE WE MOVED IN, DAD DECIDED THE INSIDE OF the new house needed to be painted. He gave his brother Wally a call, and the next day they started painting our bedroom. After a while I looked at the walls—they looked streaked and blotchy. No one could figure out why the paint job looked so bad. My Uncle Wally and father just stood there for the longest time, trying to figure it out. What had gone wrong?

This thought process went on for the longest time, until they finally decided to read the label on the paint can—something my father hadn't done when he bought the paint. He had picked up, by accident, the latest breakthrough in painting: a water-based paint that should have been mixed with water, not paint thinner. It was a new concept, because paint up until that time was made with an oil base—and, to say the least, it was messy, smelly, and hard to clean up. They had to paint the entire room over, and when it was done it looked great.

The next day Dad and Wally were out in the carport, trying to figure out how to move a dresser from inside the carport and out into the driveway. The dresser had already been loaded onto the pickup while inside the carport. When they tried to pull out, the top of the dresser stood too high—it would have hit the carport roof. My father, smart as he was, stood there with his brother; they couldn't figure out how to pull the truck out without hitting the dresser. It was funny to watch!

Finally, they decided to cut the top of the dresser off with a saw. Just before they started to saw away, I told them to stop. Remember, I was in the second grade, and they were grownups. I told them to take the dresser off the truck, pull the truck out of the carport, and reload the dresser back onto the truck. My father just stood there and looked at me for the longest time. He couldn't believe that at my age, I could solve this serious problem. All I can say is it worked. They were amazed at the simple solution. I never forgot how proud it made me feel.

The Green Monster

AT NIGHT, IT WAS NICE KNOWING THAT MY PARENTS' bedroom was right down the hall. I started out in the new house sleeping great, until Mike started telling me there was a Green Monster under my bed. He talked me into believing it. Every night, I looked under my bed, expecting this monster to reach up and grab my leg or arm and pull me under the bed and eat me. I can still remember what the monster looked like: green with big fangs. There were many nights I would leap up from my bed and run to sit by my parents' bedroom door so I would be safe from this imaginary beast. My parents would find me sleeping in front of their door in the morning. While I was sleeping in front of the door, Francois would growl at me from underneath the bed so I had to be real quiet.

Cedar Hills Park
(SUMMER 1956)

AFTER LIVING ON 123RD FOR A WHILE, ALL THREE OF us boys explored our surroundings, finding a lot to do. Just up the street was Cedar Hills Park. Back then, it was a small playground with some large swings. The swings were great for swinging and then bailing out at just the right time, seeing how far you could fly through the air and land on your feet. Sometimes you would fly too far and land face-down in the sawdust. There were also some apple trees left over from an old farm that once stood there. We would climb the apple trees to eat the green apples, and guess what? That's right! We all got serious stomachaches.

Behind the apple trees stood a large forest with tall fir trees. After a windy day, large branches would fall, and we'd use them to make big forts. There were always enough fir branches to cover the fort and to make a wonderful soft floor to lay or sit on. The forts always smelled like the forest, and even though we would come home with pitch on our hands, it was worth it. Along with making forts, we climbed the huge fir trees—all the way to the top. Sometimes we would climb so high, we would look down and not be able to see the ground. For whatever reason, I had no fear—I loved being up high. Certain trees became our lookout posts. The Geigle boys knew every inch of the woods, and were always aware of any sidewinders that would try to enter and surprise us. We even had bird calls to tell each other when intruders had entered our domain.

After we had been playing in the woods for months, one day some park workers came into the forest and cleared out a large area among the trees. To our surprise, they built a new Indian tepee, and the walls of a small log cabin. Not only had they built the tepee and log cabin, they had made trails from one end of the woods to the other.

After they had completed the trails, they constructed a building with bathrooms, a storage room, and a covered play area, on the opposite side of the woods. Under the covered play area they placed a couple of picnic tables. This was all new to us boys until it all became clear a few weeks later, when school got out for the summer. A young man and some young women would open up the new building and pull out games from the storage for us. Soon there were a lot of kids showing up. It became a place to go and have fun. We would have great summer days of softball, kickball, and paddleboard. Sometimes, we would go on bike rides through the woods, using the new trails, and even stop to play in the tepee and the log cabin.

One of the supervisors was a nice young college girl. She was a lot of fun, and liked playing all the games. I can still remember her name: Jean. I always wondered how she got one green eye and one brown eye. Jean looked after my brothers and me and kept all us kids busy and out of trouble. The park instructors made our summer days at day camp enjoyable and safe. I always thought moving to 123rd was one of the smartest things my parents did for us three boys.

Barnes Grade School
(1958)

I ENTERED BARNES GRADE SCHOOL AS A SECOND grader at nine years old. For whatever reason, I was behind in my reading and spelling, and had gained a little weight. I also had a problem with my eye shooting out whenever I looked at someone. I'm sure it looked a little weird—even today, when I look up or get really tired, my eye will start to wander. My parents took me to the eye doctor every week, where I was given eye exercises: I was supposed to move a little monkey, using my right eye, into a cage using my left. My brother Steve had the same problem with his eyes, but not as bad. Finally Steve and I both had operations to shorten our eye muscles, so our eyes wouldn't fly out when we looked at someone. The operation worked for my brother, but my eye continued to wander at times.

Because I was behind in my reading skills, I also had to have a special reading class. Words would be projected onto a screen and I would have to sound them out. These problems were not easy for me to deal with at that age. It was tough enough, as a little boy, to have to sit still in class—but having to take special classes, and then, on top of that, having an eye operation meant that it was not an easy school year. My saving grace was doing well in PE, and loving the competitive games. But sitting still was hard. I had developed a sense of humor and was good at saying things that would make the whole class laugh. I guess I loved the attention I got from being funny.

Now We're Wanted in Three States

ONE SUMMER DAY IN THE SUMMER OF 1959, MY DAD drove home in a brand-new 1959 Vauxhall station wagon, imported from Germany. Even though it was a little compact car, all three of us boys could fit in the back seat. It was light blue on the outside and dark blue on the inside. Francois, our dog, was given a spot way in the back—where he could lie down, or hang his head over the back seat. When he hung his head over the seat, his tongue would hang out, and he would start drooling all over us kids. It wasn't something I enjoyed, but we put up with it because he was a part of the family.

A few weeks later, after breaking in the new car, we all hopped in and headed down to Seaside, Oregon, for a day at the beach. Once there, we built a fire and had fun throwing the baseball around, and daring each other to go in the cold water. After a long day at the beach, we headed on home. While driving back, all of a sudden our station wagon hit something in the road and started to sound like a semi. I couldn't believe how loud it was. We immediately pulled over, and Dad crawled under the car. Sure enough, he found a hole in the muffler. A car could only be so loud—if you were too loud, you could easily get a ticket. After checking the car over, we all piled back in, and tried to continue our journey home. It seemed everyone we passed was looking at us like we were criminals and should be locked up.

As we drove noisily down the highway with the engine backfiring, a police car pulled up behind us and turned on his lights. My dad got a worried look on his face and pulled over. The officer got out of his car and walked up to the Vauxhall and said, "Good afternoon." "Good afternoon," my father replied. The officer asked him where all the noise was coming from. My father started to explain how we hit something in the road a few miles back and were just trying to make it home. In the back seat, my brother Steve, with a loud voice, said, "Oh, *great!* Now we're wanted in *three states!*"

My dad immediately turned and gave Steve his *I'm-going-to-kill-you* look, and turned back to the officer and continued to plead his case. The officer looked at my dad, and then at all three of us boys smiled at him. And with a look of pity, the officer said, "Mr. Geigle, be sure you go right home and get your muffler fixed." He also handed my dad a warning ticket, and then said, "Have a nice day." Then he gave us boys a final look, shook his head, and returned to his police car.

By the time the officer was on his way, Steve had moved back in his seat to where my dad couldn't reach while driving. We made it home. By then, Dad had calmed down, with a little help from my mother. Steve's comment became one of those family stories told over and over.

Third Grade
(1959)

I MADE IT THROUGH THE SECOND GRADE AND THEN met Mrs. Bumgardner in the third grade, when I was ten. She put a stop to me not learning, and made me bear down on my studies. Other kids went to recess, but I had to stay in class and read to her, or say my times tables. She tried to be positive and get me to concentrate. It helped, but she also knew I needed to play. When I did go to recess, I was in my zone, playing kickball on the playground. My parents would get upset when I got home because I was wearing out the toe of my right tennis shoe. I played every day, and even though I was just a third grader, I was picked by the sixth graders to be on their team. No one knew that down the road, playing kickball would lead to me playing football in high school and college.

Fifth Grade
(1961)

My last year at Barnes Grade School, I was twelve years old and in the fifth grade. Mr. Cruthers was my teacher. He took a liking to me and had a good sense of humor. I was always saying something clever in his class, making everyone laugh.

One day, Mr. Cruthers came over to me, grabbing me by the coat sleeve. He led me to the back of the room, where the coats were hanging, and lifted me up, hanging me on one of the coat hooks. Everyone went crazy with laughter as I hung there, enjoying the attention. He left me there until he was done talking.

Mr. Cruthers was a good teacher, and I think he understood how hard it was for me to sit still. Because I loved recess so much, I was always the first one out of the classroom door. When the bell rang, everyone raced to go outside. One day I had a bright idea— that ended up being one of my bad days. Since I was always the first one to the door, I thought I would fake falling down and create a big pileup. It worked—big time. Kids were falling all over the place. I was at the bottom of the pile, curled up and laughing my head off.

When the pile cleared, Mr. Cruthers picked me up and told me to come with him to the office. I was in big trouble—he didn't think what I had done was very funny.

After talking with the principal, it was decided that I had to bend over and get spanked with a yardstick. I must say: it hurt! I jumped around that office for a while with my butt stinging. I never did the door thing again, and was a little more careful about how I acted in class.

I would like to say it was my last trip to the office, but that wouldn't be true. A few weeks later, playing kickball, I got hold of one and it went through one of the classroom windows. The teacher on duty couldn't figure out how I kicked the ball so far. So there I was again, in front of the principal. I would like to say that the spanking with that yardstick stung just as bad the second time. After that, I made very sure I never returned to the principal's office again!

Snipe Hunting
(SUMMER 1961)

ONE SUMMER NIGHT, MY BROTHER MIKE, THOUGHT he would pull a fast one on us. He asked us if we wanted to go snipe hunting. Steve and I thought that would be great fun. Without even asking what a snipe was, we went along with Mike's big hunt. He told us that snipes were very fast and only came out at night, and that we would be able to catch them if we used a stick to beat the brush and a pillowcase to put the snipe in once we caught one.

Steve and I waited all day, until it was dark out. Mike led us over to a large field behind the neighbor's house across the street. He told us to start beating the high grass with our sticks, and to call out, "Here, snipe. Here, snipe." So we started our hunt. Mike continued to direct us and told us not to quit until we had one.

An hour later, we were still out in that field, beating the grass with our sticks. Mike was gone. After a while, we started to question snipe hunting. Sure enough, when we got back to the house, Mike was sitting on the porch, with a big grin on his face. We had been suckered! He asked how many snipes we got! We said, "Yeah, right!" Then we went into house, and never went snipe hunting again.

Moving to Bowmont Street

Toward the end of fifth grade, Dad announced to the family that we would be moving to a new section of Cedar Hills. We were going to build a beautiful new, split-level, four bedroom home. We were all excited, and immediately piled into the Vauxhall station wagon and headed over to SW Bowmont Street.

When we arrived, Dad pointed out where the new house would sit. He told us three boys that we would finally have our own bedrooms. The house would be more than twice as big as the place on 123rd, and would have a double garage with a long driveway for basketball. He then pointed out that the new house would be one of the first built in that section of Cedar Hills. From then on, every day when Dad got home from work, we would take a ride over to the construction site.

It took three months to build our new resort. Finally, the house was completed. As we stood in the new living room, on the afternoon the house was completed, and before moving in, we could feel the excitement. There we stood, in our brand-new home. We could smell the fresh paint on the walls, and the varnish on the hardwood floors. Every part of this house was shiny and ready for us to enjoy. On the main floor sat the living room with a corner brick fireplace. As you looked out the large back windows, there was a long sun deck under the fir trees—it ran the length of the living room. This deck was now ready for my dad's famous salmon bakes; full of laughter and fun times. Off the end of the deck, a stairway ran down to a large patio off the family room.

The dining room was upstairs, at the end of a new full-length galley kitchen that sat behind the main wall of the living room. The kitchen and dining room also had windows looking out toward the front of the house. Upstairs were three bedrooms and a large bathroom. Downstairs was a family room with another fireplace, a full bath, and one more bedroom. The good news was that Mike was going to be downstairs and I wouldn't get pushed out the window anymore. Life was good!

If you continued going down the stairs and past the family room, there was another small basement. We called it "the bomb shelter," because back then there was always the possibility of an attack by Russians.

Columbus Day Storm
(OCTOBER 12, 1962)

IN THE FALL OF 1962, MY FRIEND PAT AND I WERE walking home from school and the wind seemed to be kicking up pretty good. Then a glass truck drove down the street. We watched as it came to a stop and all the glass blew right off the truck. We were lucky the glass didn't cut us in half. At that moment we both decided it would be a good idea to get home. We walked a small distance when suddenly we stopped to watch a fence being picked up by the wind and carried off. At that point we said to each other, "See you tomorrow," and ran to our homes to get safely inside.

The storm lasted well into the night, and as I lay in my bed, hoping the wind and the sound of trees snapping would go away soon, I heard an explosion outside my bedroom window. As I opened the blinds, I saw a telephone pole catch fire. The transformer that hung on the side of the pole was shooting hundreds of sparks into the air with the sound of electricity escaping. I was pretty scared, but it was raining hard enough that after a while the fire died down and went out. That night, winds rose to 125 miles an hour, and many trees came down. Lucky for us, dad had the trees in the backyard topped, so we didn't lose any.

The next morning, when the storm was over, we came out from hiding. Debris was everywhere. The air smelled wonderful and the sun was shining brightly. Because of all the fallen trees, there was the scent of being in the woods wherever you went. For the next few days, we cooked our meals over a fire in the fireplace in our family room, which was kind of cool. We were happy when our electricity came back on. We all survived, and it didn't take long until everything was back to normal.

CHAPTER THREE
JUNIOR HIGH SCHOOL

Where Did the Little Fat Boy Go?

WHEN I WAS IN SIXTH GRADE, THE PE TEACHER announced that flag football tryouts would meet after school. Those interested in playing should meet outside the gym. I thought it would be fun to play, so after school I showed up with some of the guys to see what it was about. Even though I was a little overweight and not very tall, I thought I would be a good football player because I was strong and fast. Some kids would call me fat and I didn't like it because it made me feel bad. Most kids, however, didn't take the chance of saying something and risking getting a fat lip. They walked lightly and were careful about what they said.

Back then I really only had one friend and his name was Pat. Pat was average height and always wore a big smile from ear to ear. Every time Pat got up in front of the class to speak he would smile and I would start laughing. I mean every time. I couldn't help it. Pat would smile and I thought it made him look like a monkey. Sometimes I would stick my head in my desk and pretend to be getting some work out so Mr. Alden wouldn't see me. Pat seemed to always look right at me when he spoke. Mr. Alden would see me laughing, and sure enough, he'd send me out in the hall until Pat was done speaking. All the kids knew it was going to happen and they would all laugh when I was sent to the hall.

I'll get back to football in a moment, but first I need to talk about what happened in class one day. Dick Noren and I were in the back of the room at the paper cutter. Dick was feeding me the paper and I was pushing the handle down, cutting the paper. As Dick fed the paper I guess I wasn't paying attention and I cut the end of his thumb off. Blood started squirting everywhere. Mr. Alden saw what had happened and ran to grab Dick's thumb, or what was left of it, and applied pressure. He then led Dick up to the main office. I remember the expression on Mr. Alden's face, and it was not good.

The whole thing was quite bloody so I started cleaning the mess up. I saw the end of Dick's thumb on the counter so I picked it up and threw it in the wastebasket. Not two seconds later Mr. Alden came flying through the door, and with a frantic voice asked, "Where's Dick's thumb?" I told him I had thrown it in the wastebasket. Mr. Alden looked at me, and then dashed to the waste basket and started digging for Dick's thumb, with papers flying everywhere. The students couldn't believe what they were seeing, and I was standing there thinking my life was over. Mr. Alden found the end of Dick's thumb, put it on a paper towel, and ran out of the room like a mad scientist who was working on a scary experiment. By then, all the kids were talking about Dick's thumb, and their eyes were huge. I was sure I would be going to reform school.

We found out later that they had rushed Dick to the emergency room and sewed his thumb back on, and that he would be back in school the next day. For the rest of the year, Mr. Alden never let me near the paper cutter again. Everyone knew it had been an accident and we all lived through it. Even after many years had gone by, whenever I saw Dick, I would always want to see his thumb. Believe it or not, you couldn't even tell it had ever been in the wastebasket.

Okay, back to football practice. I got a little side-tracked. Coach put us into positions, and I ended up on the line. He explained how to run the first play. My job was to pull around the end and lead-block for the ball carrier on a sweep play. When we were all set to run the play, the center hiked the football, and away we went.

Except I went the wrong way and ran smack into the ball carrier. Well, long story short, that kid was done for the day. I hit him pretty hard. After helping the ball carrier, the coach came over to me. He said I was too rough and that I should think about playing tackle football.

I don't remember too much about playing flag football that year, but what the coach said stayed with me. I skipped football the following year—I missed the sign-up and instead used that time to deliver newspapers—and started football again in eighth grade.

My last story about the sixth grade is one that I've always laughed about. The sixth grade class was asked to put on a play for the rest of the school. In this play I was asked to be Nikita Khrushchev in a mock United Nations meeting. We decided that the play should be funny and I was to make Nikita Khrushchev's famous speech where he took off his shoe and banged it on the podium. When it came time for my speech, I took off my shoe and started to hit the podium. Suddenly, the shoe flew out of my hand and sailed off the front of the stage. Without hesitating, and to the amazement of everyone, I leapt from the stage, grabbed my shoe, and leapt back up to my position at the podium—continuing my speech like nothing had happened. The audience was in hysterics, and couldn't believe what they had just seen.

Once I had finished my speech I sat down behind the podium in a folding chair. Pat, my friend, was supposed to walk across the stage selling popcorn and peanuts, but when he came across, he accidently tripped and headed right for me. All the popcorn and peanuts went into the air, and we both went over backwards in the folding chair. The entire audience erupted in laughter, and even Mr. Alden couldn't believe what he was seeing. It was great fun. I realized I was good at making others laugh.

Summer Days
(1962–1963)

EVERY MORNING DURING THE SUMMER, I WOULD GET up early, put my baseball glove on the handlebars of my bike, and ride up to Cedar Hills grade school to practice baseball. This particular summer was different than the others, in that I seemed to be a pretty good shortstop. Instead of playing on the seventh-grade team where I belonged, the eighth-grade coach brought me up to play with the eighth-graders. The kid who had been playing shortstop didn't like the idea that a seventh grader was better than him.

One day at practice we all took a time-out to get a drink of water. We jumped on our bikes and rode down to the drinking fountain behind the school. When I got to the fountain, I waited for my turn to get a drink. I stepped up and put my head down to drink, and this kid who didn't like me playing his position shoved my head into the metal faucet and laughed. I guess he didn't know me very well, because I turned, and with one punch, hit him square in the nose, breaking it. After that, I think everyone realized I had a side to me that you didn't want to see—a result of having been called fat. That kid came back the next day with his nose taped. I never had another problem on the eighth-grade team.

William Walker Seventh Grade: The Wild Ride

I ATTENDED WILLIAM WALKER SCHOOL FOR ONE year while Meadow Park, our new junior high, was being built. William Walker had also just been built. It was a first- through eighth-grade school, but only for that year. I can remember the long hallways that sloped downhill, and the shiny new floors.

One day while I was in choir class the teacher sent me up to the library to bring back a piano (which could be rolled on wheels). When I started back with the piano, I headed down one of the sloped hallways. I got the piano going pretty fast, so I decided to hop on board this newly acquired battleship. Remember, I was just a kid having fun. I got on top of this monster and was riding it like a wild horse in a western, when all of a sudden a classroom door opened and I ran smack into it, slamming it shut with a loud bang!

I found out later, when I was standing in front of the principal telling my story, that a teacher had opened the door and was thrown back into the classroom when the piano hit it. Because I was out in the hall I knew no one really saw what had happened, so I indicated with a straight face that the piano had gotten away from me coming down the hall, and that I lost control because it was so heavy. The principal gave me a funny look for the longest time, but couldn't do anything except have me sit in the office for a while. I was really lucky. I don't remember him even telling my parents. A few weeks later I was put on a different schedule, which removed me from choir. I always thought it was because I couldn't sing—but maybe the real story got out somehow, and it was payback for my wild ride down the hall.

That year it was real hard to sit still. It seemed the teachers were always after me to pay attention. They could see I was a nice kid, and that I always made the class a little more fun with my jokes and comments. That year, kids were commenting on how I was starting to grow taller. The extra pounds were turning into muscle. In PE class, I threw the ball harder and kicked it farther. My parents were going crazy with all the food I was consuming. I would play basketball out in front of our house for hours, and then come inside to down half a gallon of milk. They got after me for wearing out my Converse tennis shoes every three weeks. Whether it was in the street playing football or in the driveway playing basketball, I loved competing.

One day in PE class we were learning to square dance. I was afraid of being paired up with Sherry Gallinger. Sherry was an aggressive redhead who had been my neighbor before we moved to Bowmont Street. We had spent many days playing in her front yard. Now she was getting older, and was very cute with her red hair and freckles. I had a major crush on her, and we teased each other a lot. She would steal my hat and run all over the playground. I could never catch her. She would give my hat back at the end of the school day and have a big laugh as she walked off.

Anyway, sure enough, we were paired up. I was dancing with her, and all of the sudden the lights in the gym started to shake and flicker. It seemed the whole gym was moving right under our feet. The teacher yelled, "Earthquake! Get against the walls." We all ran to the side of the gym and watched with fear and amazement at how the gym was rolling and moving. When it was over, we were all pretty scared. Some of the lights were still swinging.

I'll never forget the earthquake that day, and how strange it felt in the gym. Sherry and I never got to finish our dance, and we never dated, but I will always think she was pretty cool. That's all I want to say about seventh grade, except that I was happy when it was over. You know what? I can't remember learning anything from any of my teachers that year. I think it was due to my inability to focus.

Eighth Grade
(1963–1964)

By eighth grade, I had grown a bit. The little fat boy was gone. I don't know where he went, but I had gained a lot of strength and speed. I can still remember playing football on Bowmont Street, and how much fun it was to fake out the other kids who were trying to catch me. The only problem was tripping over the curbs on the end runs. Many of my afternoons in the summer were spent with the little guys in the neighborhood who would try to tackle me on the front lawn. Sometimes I would have four or five little guys on my back or around my legs, trying to take me down. I would have to maintain my balance so they wouldn't get hurt. I would walk from one end of the yard to the other. This could be where I learned balance and how not to get tackled in football. These little guys were relentless as they chased me around the yard. I would elude them; it was great fun.

The Beginning of Number 30

When summer was over, eighth grade Pop Warner Tackle Football was ready to start, so I signed up. When I told my father, he looked at me and told me I couldn't play. He said his father hadn't let him play because he might get hurt, so I couldn't play because he was afraid I would get hurt. I continued to nag at him, and finally he gave in, but told me I would have to buy my own football shoes. So I figured out a way and bought my own shoes. To this day, I can't remember where I got them. I think they were used.

So in 1963, at Barnes School, I started tackle football. Mr. Stassens was our coach, and his real estate company sponsored the team. He was a stocky six-footer, and to me he seemed huge. I learned very quickly that Coach Stassens loved football, and was tough and fair. On the first day after we warmed up and had run some drills, he decided to put me with the ball carriers. He told me I was going to be the fullback. I think he figured that out when other players would try to tackle me and I would run them over. It was a great feeling to hit someone. It seemed the harder I hit them the better it felt. Most ball carriers tried to avoid the tackler, but not me. I looked for them so I could run them over, or lower my shoulder to protect the ball and gain more yards.

That year we played nine games, and my life changed. I made many new friends and scored many touchdowns. During that time I also played defensive nose guard and made a lot of tackles, but I loved playing fullback so much I didn't realize I was becoming a very good defensive player. At the end of the season I was told by Coach Stassens that I was the best fullback he had ever coached. When he said that, my eyes lit up, and right then I decided I wanted to be a great football player. I loved the game.

By the way, my father and mother never missed a game all season. Most of the time, my father traveled from state to state for work. He would drive hundreds of miles in a single day just to watch me play. He loved it, too. Even though the fact that I was playing football frightened my mother, she enjoyed the games and going to pizza with all the parents afterwards.

During school that year I looked out the window a lot and got an A+ for day dreaming. I was good at that. I can remember the day President Kennedy was shot. One of the students laughed, and Mr. Kirkpatrick picked him up by the front of his coat and shook him. The rest of us couldn't believe that the president had been shot. Within the hour, our school was let out and closed for a few days. We all watched the constant replay of the shooting and funeral on TV with a lot of sadness. It took a long time for things to get back to normal. We all pretty much agreed that Kennedy had been a great president.

After football was over, I really wanted to play basketball, but I was afraid of going out for the team. My basketball games had been held mostly in front of my house, in the driveway. The kids who were trying out for the basketball team that year seemed to be smoother or more refined in their shooting and dribbling. I should have gone out; it was a missed opportunity. I could have helped the team. No one worked or played harder than I did. Instead, I joined the wrestling team—which was okay, I guess, although I hated rolling around on the mat and putting my face in someone else's arm pit. Even though I didn't like it, I never lost a match. I should have played basketball.

Years later, when I became a teacher and coach, parents and students would ask me about going out for a sport, or going to college, or learning to sing—they'd ask a hundred different questions about things they weren't sure if they should try. I always told them that they should try to answer the question for themselves or they might regret it their whole life. Some parents try to answer the question for their kids, telling them they can't try this because they don't want them to get hurt or they want them to try something else. Big mistake. Your kid may end up resenting you forever. If you think you or your child would like to try something, then go ahead and give it try. Even if you only try it for a short time and decide it's not for you, at least you've answered the question and can move on.

Okay, back to the eighth grade. One of my worst moments that year was when I was walking down the hall and happened to look in a classroom where, to my amazement, I saw Nanci, who I thought was my girlfriend, sitting on Gordi's lap. Gordi was one of my best friends. Nanci had a big smile on her face until she saw me. I couldn't believe what I was seeing. I went over and grabbed Gordi; dragged him out into the hall and started to whale on him.

Mr. Kirkpatrick saw us and came rushing over. He grabbed both of us by our collars and banged our heads together like a couple of rag dolls. I think it almost knocked both of us out. Then he dragged us down to the office, where we sat and waited for the principal. When I turned and looked at Gordi, he turned and looked at me, and we both started to laugh. I'll never forget that day and how it made me feel. I guess I took that situation a little too seriously; it bothered me for a long time. I didn't speak to Nanci for a whole year, and when I did talk to her it was too late, for I had already met another girl, also named Nancy.

My Childhood Sweetheart
(SUMMER 1964)

IN THE SUMMER OF 1964, I WAS AT THE NEIGHBOR-hood baseball field, sitting in the bleachers watching the baseball It was one of those hot summer nights that we all remember, with the warm breeze cooling our skin, and the smell of freshly cut grass filling our senses. I was fifteen years old and full of myself. I was strong, steady, and confident. Looking back, I guess I'd have to say I was a pretty good catch with my healthy summer tan and a carefree attitude.

As I was sitting there, two girls came up and sat down in front of me. Being the ham I was, I started kidding with them and asking who they were. One girl was Nancy Holland. She had beautiful brown eyes that twinkled. When she looked at me and smiled, that was all it took—she had me. She was tan with long brown hair, and only a little over five feet tall. The thing was, when I kidded with her, she would kid me right back, and we would all laugh. Her friend Becky was also cute and fun, but there was something special about Nancy.

By the time the game was over, Nancy and I were sitting next to each other, not caring or paying attention to anything going on around us. When the game was over, I asked if I could walk her home. As we walked, there was a certain strange feeling or energy between us, and we just kept smiling and walking. By the time we walked up to her front door I looked at her and asked if she would go steady with me. She said yes, so I said good night. I didn't see her again for the rest of that school year—because I was a freshman at Sunset High School and she was still at Meadow Park Junior High, our worlds were just too far apart at that time. However, we would meet again. The next school year, I was a sophomore and Nancy entered Sunset High as a freshman. During the first few days of school, we happened to run into each other in the hallway. Once again, that great smile and the twinkle in her eyes knocked me over. We exchanged greetings and kidded for a moment, and I said, "Hey! By the way, are we still going steady?" She smiled and said, "Of course!" For the next three years there was hardly a day we weren't together.

We spent a lot of time at Nancy's house. I really enjoyed her family. Ernie was her younger brother, who wanted to know everything about everything, and followed me around wherever I went. During the summer I would go to baseball practice, and Ernie would come with me. When we arrived at the practice he would take a seat on the bleachers. When practice was over he would follow me home, asking a hundred questions and talking all the way. Ernie went on to become a great man, full of success and ambition. Years later, I saw him on a reality TV show, hunting bear in Alaska. Even though it had been years since I had seen him, I could still see the ambitious young boy I had known so many years before.

Nancy's other younger brother, Eddie, was funny and full of crazy ideas. He was into everything and everyone's business. One night Nancy and I were sitting on the couch watching a movie in her living room when we couldn't believe what we saw. Eddie, still a young boy, was walking in his sleep; he had walked down the main hall from his bedroom and into the living room. He started peeing into one of the large flower pots in the corner of the room. I don't think I ever laughed so hard. Nancy jumped up from the couch and let out a scream as she ran after Eddie. She grabbed him and led him to the bathroom to make sure he was aimed right. He was still just a little guy then, and a lot of fun to be around.

Jasper and Bessy were Nancy's parents. Jasper was a respected geologist, and Bessy was a wonderful lady who stayed home and raised all six kids. You could hear Bessy from one end of the house to the other calling everyone for dinner, or barking out a command to Jasper to control the boys from fighting or get them to the dinner table. I can hear her voice even today, yelling, "Jasper, it's time for dinner! You better get in here—Jasper, where are you? Get those boys in here. It's time for dinner. Nancy, is Larry staying for dinner? Larry, get yourself around the table!" There we were, all huddled around a small table in the kitchen, with at least six or seven people eating fried chicken or whatever.

One night Nancy thought she would surprise me with a banana cream pie. When she brought me a piece, the pie was pretty good except she had forgotten the bananas. We all had a pretty good laugh about that. Even now it makes me chuckle. I never could understand what she did with the bananas.

Nancy's family lived in a three bedroom ranch home and raised all six kids in that little house. Ernie and Eddie were in one bedroom, and Annette and Nancy were in another; Norma and Nelda had already married and were out of the house. I was there so much that one would have thought I was part of the family. These were great people and a solid part of my young life. I'll never forget those days with Nancy and her family. Jasper and Bessy never moved from that house. Many years later, I stopped by and said hello—the house had remained the same.

During the school year I asked Nancy to go to the Christmas formal. It was her first high school dance and she was pretty excited. During this week of excitement and getting ready for the dance, Nancy told me she had to collect samples for a science project. She asked if I would help her go into the woods and collect these important specimens. At that time we had forest all around us, so it wasn't hard to find trees with lots of collectibles. Of course, I was the one doing the collecting, while she stood and pointed out what she wanted collected. Well, good ol' Nancy had me pick up something interesting, and then realized that it was poison oak! "You'd better put it down," she said, but it was too late. Twenty-four hours later I'm standing in her living room with my face covered with masses of rash, on the way to the Christmas formal. Nancy looked great, and I looked like a pomegranate ready to be eaten.

After the dance I took her to a nice restaurant in downtown Portland. She ordered a Crab Louie salad. She didn't know she was allergic to crab. A few minutes passed before she started reacting. Ten minutes later, her face was starting to look like a beach ball, getting bigger. I thought it would be a good idea to get her home. It turned out to be quite a night, with my poison oak and her crab reaction. But it was always special to be with her, and we had some good fun.

Chapter Four

MY FATHER AND BROTHERS

My Dad: Hughbert Leon Geigle

MY FATHER WAS A GREAT MAN, WITH A GREAT sense of humor that brought with it a wonderful laugh and smile. Most people liked and respected him and were better off for knowing him. Dad was born in 1925, in the small town of Skeeter, North Dakota. When he was a young boy, his mother and father decided to pack up the Model T and move to the St. Johns area of Portland, Oregon. Dad would meet my mother, Iva June, in the summer of 1944. Their love affair lasted more than fifty years.

My father's sales career started as a teenager during the depression. He and his two brothers, Del and Wally, would make beer in the basement of my grandmother's house and sell it to the merchant marine sailors coming to Portland. Times were tough back then, and Dad would tell us boys how he would play his guitar and sing on the radio on the weekends. He would receive a couple of bucks and two free movie tickets to take my mother to a movie on Saturday night. As time went by and we three boys came along, he took a job working at Nordstrom. After working hard, he emerged as one of Nordstrom's top managers. After years of success at Nordstrom, Dad became the vice president of the Bon Marche Shoe Division, in Seattle, Washington. Toward the end of his career, he left Seattle and came back to Portland. He developed and opened a new store for Nordstrom, known as Nordstrom Rack.

Dad was an excellent golfer, poker player, and fisherman . . . just ask him. On the weekends, you would find him down at Sauvie Island on Marshall Beach, sitting in his folding chair, spitting sun flower seeds and waiting for the next run of fish to come up the Columbia River. We three boys would be with him, playing along the beach, waiting for the next ship to roll by and make its monster waves, or cleaning fish for the older fisherman who needed help. Mother would be lying on a blanket, in the warm sand, reading a new thriller and soaking up the sun, or huddled over the fire, cooking.

Our freezer would be full of fish that Dad had caught, waiting to be cooked at the next "Hugh Geigle Luau." His luaus weren't small; there could be fifty to a hundred people, all from the shoe business, on the beach at one time. There were plenty of fish stories, laughter, jokes and good times. It was a great way to spend summer days at the river.

I always enjoyed the hot summers; swimming, playing on the beach, my father catching salmon and cooking them out on the back deck at home. Our house on Bowmont Street was a new, custom-built home, situated on a lot which had beautiful fir trees. The trees helped keep us cool by providing shade, and provided us with the constant scent of being in the forest. We spent most of our hot summer nights sleeping in the backyard, under the trees, in sleeping bags. I don't think my brother Steve slept in his bed the whole summer.

My Brother: Steven Jay Geigle

STEVE WAS THE MIDDLE SON OF THE THREE BOYS IN the family. When he put his mind to something, you knew that you might just as well get out of the way. He was a Geigle all the way, especially when it came to getting it done. Steve loved astronomy, and demonstrated it by building a telescope, from scratch, in our living room, and then standing out in the front yard on a hot summer night, gazing up into the heavens, and looking at the different constellations. He was always happy to explain the total solar system to anyone who passed by and would listen—especially the pretty girls in the neighborhood.

Steve was a very talented musician, and would sit down at the piano or strap on a guitar and play the latest hit songs. Most of the time, however, he would play his drums, trying to come up with a new beat—all without any lessons. He played by ear, and it was all pretty impressive. Later, in high school, he would form a rock group which he named "Big G and the Cheerios." This group consisted of five high-school friends: Greg, Roger, Jim, my brother Steve, and myself on bass guitar. The band was fun, and even though I had to drop out because of football, we continued to play for the high school dances and events around the community.

One of the funniest stories about my brother Steve was about how he was determined to invent the first hover craft, or flying machine, using a plywood base and a lawnmower engine for its propulsion system. The hover craft was a simple design. It looked like a round table-top with an old kitchen chair sitting in the middle, and the engine mounted underneath. Steve told us he was going to steer the hover craft by simply leaning to the right to go right, and leaning left to go left. In theory it sounded good, but in reality this was a young kid spitting in the wind, as they say.

When the hover craft was ready for its maiden voyage, Steve sat in the pilot seat and gave the start cord a pull. It fired right up, and then immediately started to vibrate. In fact, it vibrated so hard that it slid across the garage floor, bouncing Steve around and then crashing into the wall, almost knocking him out of the pilot seat. Steve looked at us with a frightened expression, and went for immediate engine shut down. That was the end of the hover craft! He got out of the craft, gave us an "Oh, well!" and never talked about it again.

First-Born: Mike Hubert Geigle

MIKE WAS THE OLDEST OF US THREE BOYS, AND WAS the outdoorsman. He loved to fish with our Dad and was always ready for a new "fishin' adventure." If you were to walk into our garage, back on Bowmont, you would never really know what to expect. Mike might have a beaver skin, deer, or who-knows-what hanging from the ceiling. Mike was a hunter and fisherman, all the way, and there have been many funny stories told about his efforts to bring home dinner from a day in the woods, or the banks of some river.

Telling this next story about Mike, I would like you to keep this in mind: Mike had to put up with his two little brothers, and sometimes I think we irritated him pretty good.

One day, when I was in the third grade, I was bothering Mike, and he was giving me the look that said, "Back off." I kept pushing my luck, so Mike started to run after me. Whenever this happened, I always had one place I could run to and hide. We had a 1953 DeSoto that no one drove anymore sitting in the driveway. At times like this, I would run for the DeSoto and jump inside. I always had one door unlocked, in case I needed it for this type of emergency. Anyway, Mike was chasing me, so I ran for the DeSoto and jumped inside, locking the door behind me. As I looked out the window, I could see my brother standing there. His lip was quivering, which meant he was mad. He walked off, and after a while I opened the door, got out, and started for the house. Then I saw Mike out of the corner of my eye, running full speed toward me. I ran to the back door of our house and went inside, slamming and locking the door behind me. As I was standing there, safely inside, I watched Mike approach. When he got to the door he stuck his arm right through the glass in it's window and grabbed me by the throat. My mother couldn't believe what she was seeing. She yelled at Mike to let me go. Blood from his arm started squirting out like a major break in a water pipe. He had a serious cut. My mother grabbed a towel and started to wrap Mike's arm, but in a panic she had started to wrap the wrong arm. My mother suddenly realized what she had done and quickly unwrapped the towel, trying again on the bleeding arm. She then led Mike over to the neighbor's house. My mother yelled at me to stay in the house, saying that she and the neighbors would be taking Mike to the hospital.

I thought for sure I had killed my brother! Hours later, when they got back, Mike had received a number of stitches in his arm. I had been crying for a long time. I was pretty scared and felt really bad. I don't think I ever teased him again. I guess it was a good lesson for both of us.

One summer day Mike brought home a go-cart. He pulled it into the garage and we all gathered around this fine machine, anticipating the fun rides around the neighborhood. But for the time being it appeared to be in pretty bad shape. Mike went in the house and brought our dad out, and started to run down a list of reasons we should keep it. Dad had a stern look on his face. He listened for a short period of time, and said, "It's a piece of junk. Get it out of here." He walked back into the house.

We all looked at each other, and Mike said, "We'll fix it up and bring him back for a second look." I think Mike had already bought the thing and couldn't take it back. All day we worked on cleaning it up. We took it apart, sanding it and painting it, and giving it a fresh spark plug. I thought it looked brand new. When it was done, we all waited for Dad to come out and take a second look. Somehow Mike got him to come back out for a second evaluation. Dad stood there, eyes fixed over the go-cart. That's when Mike decided to start it up. Dad came closer, and when Mike tried to pull the start cord, all of a sudden there was a huge bang and a large cloud of grey smoke, with the smell of gas and exhaust. We all jumped back and stood silent. Then we saw what had happened. We had forgotten to tighten down the spark plug. The spark plug was now missing and my dad had been thrown back against the garage wall with a startled look on his face. We started looking around for the spark plug and couldn't find it until we all looked up at the ceiling. There the spark plug hung, embedded into the ceiling's dry wall. Dad turned and glared at us and made his way back to his easy chair in the house. He never said another word about the go-cart.

CHAPTER FIVE

HIGH SCHOOL

The Start of High School Football
(1964–1965)

GOING BACK... 1964 WAS THE START OF MY
freshman year of high school, and my first of high school football.
Our coach was Dan Hess. Not only was he our coach but our history
teacher as well. Coach Hess was tough in the classroom as well as on
the field; he always walked around with a stern look on his face. He
was about five foot ten, medium build, and had played football and
wrestled in high school and college. Because we had been undefeated
the season before, he and everyone else expected us to be good again.

Coach Hess wanted to find out what we were made of, so for
the first practice, we ran a machine-gun drill. That's where the
team makes a long single line and one player at a time runs and
attacks the other player, who is standing five yards away. One at

a time, they attack you until they knock you out of your position. The player being attacked shucks the oncoming player to one side or another and maintains his position. Guess who was first to be machine-gunned? When I had gone through the entire team and was still standing there, waiting for another attacker, I could see the coach with a kind of a grin on his face. I always loved that drill. It's where I gained a lot of respect, very quickly.

After a few weeks of practice we were boarding the bus to play our first game with Central Catholic, and Coach Hess got on the bus, standing in front with a hat on. He told us that he had never lost a game when wearing his lucky hat. Guess what? We lost the game. In fact, we got killed! I don't think we understood the plays yet, and our timing was off. Coach Hess never wore his hat again, and we never lost another game that year.

Because our games were on Saturday mornings, we would play football, then all show up at the Beaverton movie theater in the afternoon, sit with our girlfriends and have kissing contests. Kirk Graves was always the winner. I was always too shy, but the popcorn was good, and drinks were cheap back then. The movie was only seventy-five cents to get in, and a popcorn ten cents, along with a drink for five cents. For a dollar you could have a whole afternoon of entertainment. It would include two one-and-a-half-hour movies and a couple of cartoons. We all had a great time on Saturdays, and it was a great way to rest from the aches and pains of playing a football game earlier that morning.

Sophomore Year
(1965-66)

AT THE END OF THE FOOTBALL SEASON I STARTED thinking about making varsity the next year as a sophomore.

Without me knowing it, my father had talked with Coach Hess after the season was over, and told him that if I asked about playing varsity the next year, he should tell me I was too small. So that's what Coach Hess told me when I asked. My dad knew exactly what he was doing, and he knew I would work even harder to make the team. He was right—I made varsity with six other sophomores the following year.

Our high school had just hired a new football coach by the name of Mouse Davis, who was developing a new offense called the "run and shoot." Playing high school football for Coach Davis in 1966 was fun and exciting. He was like a maverick and you never knew what to expect. Mouse had a great personality, and not only inspired his players, but our entire high school. He was the first coach to start a winning season at Sunset High School.

Playing for Mouse as a sophomore, I kicked off and punted, and spent time learning the plays at running back and nose guard. Mouse always kept us seven sophomores close to him so he could groom us into his way of football.

One of the memories I have of 1966 is one particularly big senior from Hillsboro High School, hitting me on a kickoff—so hard that I ended up under the bleachers, and out for the season with a split sternum. The other players had great fun kidding with me by poking my chest so they could watch me go down to my knees in pain. That was the way guys dealt with each other. It took me a long time to heal, but when I did I was ready to pay Hillsboro back for the pain they had inflicted on me. That first year with Coach Davis, we had a winning season, and looked forward to the next year of football and playing for our new coach.

The Big Takeover
(1966-67)

WHEN THE 1967 FOOTBALL SEASON ROLLED AROUND, I was ready for "the big take-over." Sometime during the last school year I had decided to take on the fullback position and also be the starting nose guard. The first few days of practice were crucial for me to win those two positions. My moment came on the second day of practice, when we were running plays.

Everyone thought Frank would be the next fullback, because he was a senior, and it was his turn. Coach called a scramble-right pass, where the fullback blocks the defensive end. Frank's team ran the play first, and his block was average and not that impressive. Then it was my team's turn to run the same play. The ball was hiked and I headed for the defensive end at full speed. When I arrived, I knocked down the defensive end with the (soon to become famous) "Geigle Forearm." You could hear the groans from the other players when the defensive man went down and didn't get up for a while. The coaches looked at each other. They didn't say much, but I could see the expressions on their faces. Coach Davis then spoke up and told me to change teams. He called for a fullback off-tackle play, and I was to get the ball. I don't know what got into me, but when I got the ball, I ran down the field for forty yards, with players trying to tackle me. I either dodged them or ran over the top of them like I was some prehistoric animal looking for my next meal. Once again the coaches didn't say anything, but I knew I had done the job, and the "little fat boy" was gone forever. The next day I was moved to the starting unit, and became the starting fullback and nose guard from that day on.

I'll never forget that year because we became such a good football team. Coach Davis would give me the ball on that off-tackle play over and over. One night in the pouring rain, I ran like a plow horse for 175 yards in the mud, in a game against Centennial High School.

I received the game ball handed to me by Coach Davis. It was a great night for our team. I couldn't help thinking I was starting to become a good fullback, and was very proud of what I had done. At the end of the season I ended up as the leading scorer for Sunset. But when the all-league selections came out, to my surprise, I was selected second team all-league on defense, not offense. On defense, I had led the team in tackles and had become a tough nose guard—but I loved fullback so much that I hadn't really thought about how I was playing as a nose guard. Shortly after the league selection came out, I started receiving recruitment letters from the University of Oregon, Oregon State, the University Of Washington, and Washington State. Oregon State invited me down for their spring scrimmage to meet the coach and players and have a nice lunch. Later that spring, I went down to Oregon State. I went into their locker room after the scrimmage and was blown away by the size of the players. When I left, I thought I might be too small to play division one football.

JV Basketball Sunset High
(1967)

WHEN FOOTBALL ENDED THAT YEAR, I HAD ALREADY decided that I wanted to play high school basketball. I loved basketball, though I hadn't developed the skills and was behind the other players. Everyone knew I wasn't a basketball player and that I looked more like a wrestler. I was constantly asked if I was going out for wrestling. I went to the basketball coach and told him I wanted to play. I told him if the team had fifteen players, I would be happy to be number sixteen. If someone was sick or got hurt, then I could fill in. I also said that if I didn't play in the games that would be okay, and that I just wanted to be part of the team. I think he liked my attitude, so guess what? I made the team.

That year, I was on the junior varsity basketball team, and if the coach needed tough defense, he would put me in to harass the other team and steal the ball. I can remember my first shot in the gym at Hillsboro High School. It was a hook shot from the top of the key. When I took the shot, the ball hit so hard, the rim fell to the floor. They had to stop the game and put a new rim on. I got ribbed by the other players quite a bit about that shot. It was great fun and I loved playing basketball that year.

Baseball at Sunset High
(1965-68)

My junior year, I went out for baseball and made the varsity team as the starting catcher. I didn't play freshman baseball because my grades weren't that great.

My sophomore year I played catcher for the JV team, but was not very impressed with the coach. I recall being bored with practice one day, when I spotted a load of sand that had been delivered down on the lower baseball diamond. After catching a ball, I put it in my glove instead of throwing it back. I then headed toward the sand pile. I sat down and started playing in the wet sand. I decided I would sculpt a naked woman. The coach saw me sitting on the pile and came down and asked me what I was doing. I stood up, looked at him, handed him the baseball, and said, "I quit." I then walked to the dressing room, got dressed, and went home. That was the end of sophomore baseball for me.

For me to feel and act like that was irresponsible, I know, but I was young, and I was making a statement: this coach had taught me to hate baseball, and I didn't ever want to play again. He didn't have the personality to be a baseball coach, and didn't know how to make it fun or worth the effort. Practices were terribly boring. All I could do was feel disrespectful toward him. I was happy that sophomore baseball was over, and that this coach was out of my life.

My junior year, our newly hired varsity baseball coach was a good ballplayer who had just graduated from the University of Oregon. He was a good player at Oregon, but once again, not a real strong personality for coaching. But he knew baseball, and after a while, you could see that even though he was young, he had potential.

As a junior, I made the varsity team as a catcher. Even though my hitting was off I always seemed to get one base. We won some games but I don't remember us being that good.

When it was my turn to play catcher, some of the football coaches would come out to the baseball games and sit in the bleachers, watching the other teams try to steal home. Back then, there were some pretty good collisions at home plate, and they knew they might see the famous "Geigle Forearm". When we played a game at Beaverton High School that year, even the Sunset football coaches drove over, crossing the railroad tracks to BHS so they could watch the big game between the Beavers and the Apollos. It was a nice day for baseball, and the bleachers were filled with students, teachers, and parents watching their team compete for bragging rights, while catching up on the latest gossip.

The Beaverton first baseman was the principal's son, Steve. He stood about six foot seven and was full of himself, but still a pretty nice guy. Toward the middle of the game, he was on third base, and I was behind home plate, catching for the Apollos. The Beavers' coach decided to have his big first baseman steal home. Everyone in the park knew it was coming. When he headed for home, he found out the hard way that it was a bad mistake. Steve was tall and came in at full speed, like a runaway freight train down the side of a mountain. I could see the determination in his eyes. When we met, I had no trouble delivering the "Geigle Forearm" to his mouth, knocking out his front teeth and sending him flying toward the dugout. Once again, as in football practice, there were groans from the people watching. Steve was called out. I felt bad for hurting him, but at that time, that's the way we played the game. After the dust had cleared, I could see my football coaches shaking their heads, confirming that the "little fat boy" was no more. The word got out, and for the rest of the season not too many more teams tried to steal home.

I didn't know it at the time, but Ad Rutschman, the Hillsboro football and baseball coach, was keeping an eye on me for the future. He would soon become the new football and baseball coach at Linfield College in McMinnville, Oregon, and was considering recruiting me to play football or baseball for the Wildcats. I had grown to admire Ad Rutschman as a coach, as well as the teams he produced.

Senior Year
(1967-68)

I'M SORRY TO SAY THAT ALTHOUGH MY SENIOR YEAR should have been my best year, it ended up as something of a disappointment. My father had become the vice president of Bon Marché's shoe division in Seattle, Washington. My parents sold our house on Bowmont Street, and we left good old Cedar Hills, moving to Seattle. I didn't realize the effect it would have on my young life and my last year of high school. I had to say goodbye to everyone—including my childhood sweetheart, Nancy; Coach Davis; football; and everything I had known and achieved. Coach Davis wasn't very happy about the move, and my relationship with Nancy had already started to erode. Neither of us had really dated anyone else, and now I'm not so sure it was a good idea to be so serious at such a young age. I said my goodbyes and loaded up my '55 Chevy convertible (what a sweet ride!) and headed toward North Gate, in Seattle, Washington, where I would attend Ingraham High School—a highly respected football school. My parents had already rented a mid-century house that was kind of cool but seemed strange and different.

The day after I got there I went over to the high school to meet the football coach and have a look at the school. The coach was nice, but I could tell he wasn't a Mouse Davis. Walking around the school, it appeared to me that it was pretty old. The hallways were dark and depressing compared to the brand-new Sunset High, which had been dubbed "the Country Club." After coming home from my visit, I was pretty depressed. I realized I didn't know anyone, and thought I would have to start all over to prove myself, and that it was going to screw up my chances of playing football in college. I decided to tell my parents that I wanted to finish school at Sunset and live with my grandmother until graduation. My parents agreed, so I packed up my '55 Chevy and headed back to Beaverton. I can still remember driving down I-5 with the top down, and the warm sun hitting me in the face. It was once again a great day, and my depression was gone. I had made the right choice.

When I arrived, Coach Davis was happy to hear the good news about my return. I was looking forward to another great season of football at Sunset Apollo. Things started to get better and my parents ended up renting an apartment for me across the street from the high school. They would come down on Friday afternoons and stock the fridge with food. They'd see the game that night, and head home again on Sunday. This lasted the whole football season. Nancy took me back and things looked pretty good. Being a senior, I had gained another ten pounds; I weighed 190 and stood a stocky five foot eight.

But unfortunately, because of all the changes in my life, I had lost a step. Things weren't quite the same. The Apollos ended up having a great season that year. I had some great games—but also some that were not-so-great. There was something missing. I think I missed the house I had grown up in and my everyday routine on Bowmont Street. My life just wasn't the same! Even though Sunset was in a tough metro league, we racked up seven wins, one loss, and one tie, missing the state playoffs to the Hillsboro Spartans once again. When the all-league selections came out, I had only made second team all-league. That was a real disappointment. I had a couple of bad games, which I knew hurt my chances—along with not being as fast or strong that season. I also knew that I was not eating right (after all, I was an eighteen-year-old living alone), and that also had something to do with the way I played.

After football season was over, my parents got rid of the apartment, and I moved in with my grandmother, driving across Portland to school for the rest of the year. Every morning I would go to the basement of her two-story boarding house and take a shower in what seemed to be sub-zero temperatures. My grandmother was a tough, wonderful, sweet German woman who loved her grandchildren. She always made sure I had plenty of French toast before I left for school, and money in my pocket for an emergency.

Even though my last days at Sunset were less-than-perfect, being with my friends made it tolerable. That spring I played baseball. I still couldn't hit the ball, but no one stole home. I graduated from Sunset by the skin of my teeth. I'll never forget my graduation present: a new Wilson catcher's mitt. My father had always wanted me to be a catcher, and he wanted me to keep playing. Back in the day, he had been a semi-pro pitcher. When we were little, he would tether us three boys to the fence or a tree, and tell us to watch the game—so we did. He was a left-handed pitcher—a "southpaw"—and pitching at the side of our house one day, threw the ball so hard it went through the side of the house. We found it in the cupboard, next to a box of Wheaties. I love that story and my father; I'll never forget him.

My senior year, Nancy and I were still dating, but she was going to be at Sunset the next year, and once again our worlds were growing apart. I was leaving high school and moving on. Nancy was voted Homecoming Queen her senior year, and won many honors. She was a very special girl, particularly to me. But I still wasn't done playing college football. I think back now how far the little fat boy had come, and how once again he would be starting all over, still excited for the future.

6

CHAPTER SIX
VIETNAM

On the Road to College
(1968-69)

IN 1968 I HAD JUST GRADUATED FROM SUNSET
High School, and wondered what my next opportunity would be.
Playing college football was my goal. One day at summer baseball
practice, a friend by the name of Eddie approached me with Stan,
who was another friend, and asked if they could talk with me. Stan
and Eddie said they were headed to the other side of Portland to
meet with Eddie's college football coach, from Columbia Basin
Junior College, in Pasco, Washington. They wanted me to ride along
and visit with him.

When practice was over, we all jumped in my '55 Chevy and
headed across town to sit with the coach and talk about the future. This coach was a nice enough guy, and made playing for the

Hawks at Columbia Basin sound pretty good. I wasn't sure about being around Eddie or Stan. They didn't seem to care about me that much. My experience with these guys had not always been positive, but it seemed they had a lot of respect for my athletic ability. After a long conversation, the coach asked Stan and I to come over to the CBC and walk on. He told us that if we made the team he would provide us with a football scholarship that would cover tuition and books. He would also provide a part-time job to supplement housing and meals. I wasn't too excited about the idea of living with Stan and Eddie, but I would be in college and get another chance to play football.

In late August we all jumped in my '55 Chevy (again, what a sweet ride!), loaded her up and headed for Pasco, Washington, home of the Columbia Basin Hawks. I was excited and ready to play some football. Stan had played defensive end and split end for Sunset, and Eddie was a linebacker and offensive guard. Eddie was tough as nails, and Stan was so tall he would overpower players with his height.

So we said goodbye to Sunset High and headed up I-84 through the Columbia Gorge. When we arrived, it was late afternoon and warm, with a gentle breeze blowing across the football field. Practice was to start the next day. When I looked around, I saw some players standing around a garbage can by the locker room. One of the players was bending over the can, and all his hair was being cut off. Eddie saw me looking at this and told me it was a tradition. All CBC football players got their hair cut off before the first practice. Then everyone in the college and around town would know you played football for the Hawks. So guess what? That's right! A few minutes later, all my hair was gone. I looked like I was in boot camp.

After throwing the football around, we hopped back in the '55 Chevy and went to a small house that Eddie had lined up for us. We got settled in and tried to get a good night's sleep before the first practice.

Practice started the next day and I found out the difference between high school players and college players. College players had a special talent, or they wouldn't be there. Even though it was my first year, I claimed the starting defensive nose guard position and second-string fullback after a few days of practice. I wanted the fullback position but there was a huge player by the name of Henry Roch. Henry stood six foot four and 250 pounds, and had started at the fullback position the year before for the Hawks. I found

Henry to be full of himself, and waited for an opportunity to take him down a notch. It happened late in the first week of practice.

Coach called for a dive play right over the center into my hole and announced it to the whole world. Of course Henry laughed and said, "That rookie can't stop me!" I didn't say anything, but when the ball was hiked and Henry came through the line into my hole, I could hear the groans from the rest of the team as he was in the air—upside down and coming down for a hard landing. I had hit him in the legs and he'd been launched into the air upside down, to the amazement of the rest of the team and coaches. Henry had just met number 30! When Henry got up he was really mad. A few choice words came out of his mouth. In the locker room, he was still mad, and almost pulled the shower head off the wall, and a few more choice words came out. That one play had sent a message to the rest of the team, and generated a large amount of respect toward me from players and coaches. I had earned my scholarship that practice—as well as a starting position for the CBC Hawks.

Four weeks later, we were still undefeated in league play, and I was being talked about in the Pasco newspaper as a potential first-year all-American in junior college. I was doing well—but also not so well. Things on the field were going well, but off the field, not so good. Because I didn't have a lot of food money, I lived on tuna fish and crackers. Twice a week I went to dinner at a restaurant where you could eat all you wanted for a dollar ninety-nine. The rest of the week, I starved. I also got tired of living with Stan and Eddie, and dealing with their wild party life. I acquired a bedroom in the basement of a house closer to campus. But it was cold and damp, and I didn't get a lot of sleep.

For the fifth game of the season we played Taft Junior College out of California, who at that time were considered a powerhouse team in the Golden Bear State. Their players were huge, and they were used to winning. We were underdogs, and not expected to win. But we showed up with a different idea in mind. We were winning—in fact, we were killing this team and loving every minute of it. Then, sometime during the third quarter, I got extremely tired, and was helped off the field. I stayed out the rest of the game. I couldn't figure out why I was getting so tired. I did notice that my throat was a little sore, but it didn't seem that bad.

The next week of practice, I realized something was wrong. For the next game, we traveled to Grays Harbor, Washington. It was a cold, wet night on the coast. During the game, I had a bad sore throat, and started spitting up blood. Also, Henry, our fullback, got hurt—so not only was I playing nose guard, I was running the ball too. I finished the game, but was in bad shape on the ride back to Columbia Basin.

I ended up going to the doctor the next day. After the doctor did a blood test he told me some bad news. I had mononucleosis. I guess I had gotten pretty run-down from not sleeping a lot, and then eating tuna fish and crackers. Or maybe it was the girl I kissed at McDonald's. Maybe I should have gotten her name before I got so friendly—but that's another story! The doctor said football was over for that year, and that I would be okay if I got complete rest. I turned in my gear, dropped out of Columbia Basin, and went home to Gramma Geigle's. If there was any place I would heal, it would be there.

My dreams of being a small college all-American drifted away. *My first attempt at college has failed*, I thought to myself. I stayed in bed for the next few weeks, and slowly started to feel better as my hair grew back. A few months later, a package came in the mail. Inside was a new Columbia Basin blue-and-white letterman's coat. It was beautiful, and I thought that was pretty neat of the coach. I wore that coat for many years, and remembered my short time as a Hawk. Nancy was back in my life, but only part-time. She was busy with school, so our relationship was somewhat distant. She had traveled a few times with my parents to Columbia Basin to watch me play, and on Saturday nights I had driven all the way home to Beaverton to see her, and all the way back to school on Sunday afternoons. I can remember the long drives, listening to the '55 Chevy purr down the highway at sixty-five miles an hour, to get me to her house safely. As I drove, I would think about how hard it had been without my parents. With them still living in Seattle, I never really felt at home, or grounded. I missed my house on Bowmont, and the warm summer days playing in the front yard. I also missed the Friday night football games at Sunset, and my old coach, and the way things used to be. I guess the '55 Chevy was like a friend or home that traveled wherever I went, and was there for me whenever I needed her. When I started that car up and heard the rumble of the exhaust and smelled the distinct odor of the '55, and then sat inside, looking at how clean she was, I guess I felt a little safer. I guess I knew there was a part of my life that hadn't changed.

United States Navy
(1969–70)

In January of 1969, I entered Portland Community College and took an advanced basketball class to get back in shape. I was feeling much better—recovering from mono and starting to feel like my old self! I ran hard in class, and it felt good to be back in shape.

During that time, I received a letter from the draft board to report for a physical. Earlier in my story, in September of 1968, I had just left with Eddie and Stan for Columbia Basin and had omitted telling about my draft physical, which occurred the same day we loaded up the '55 Chevy and headed for football try-outs. As the story goes, earlier that morning, before we left for try-outs, I went down to the draft board to be tested and have a physical. Back then, if you weren't a full-time student, you could receive a draft classification number and be called up to serve, according to your number. When I went down to Portland for the physical, they were very impressed with my physical condition and told me that they would like to test me to see where I would do well in the military. I told them I didn't have time and that it would make me late. I tried to explain that I was headed to college that day, and would take the test later. They insisted that I stay and take the test before I left. I said, "Okay. Give me the test." I sat down and took the test, marking the answers without even reading the questions. They were surprised to see how fast I had finished, and sent me on my way, shaking their heads as I left.

Months later, I received a letter from the draft board. College wasn't going as planned, and I wasn't a full-time student—so I was worried about being drafted. I thought I had better go down to the Navy recruiter and see what my options were. Both of my brothers were in the Navy and still alive, so I thought it might be a good direction for me. After talking with the recruiter I came away somewhat upset. My test scores were some of the lowest he had ever seen. It didn't surprise me, but he indicated that my only option would be a four-year enlistment as a deck hand on a Naval ship. Before I left, I told him that if a program came up where I could do two years active duty, I would sign up. He told me there was no such program, so I left. I went back to Gramma Geigle's and thought to myself, "What should I do next?" After two weeks of sitting around thinking of what to do, I received a letter from the Navy recruiter. It said I could serve for two years active duty and four years in the inactive reserve. I would also receive the GI Bill, which would allow me to return to college. This sounded pretty good, and would give me a chance to return to college and play football one more time. I had already decided to attend Linfield College when I returned from active duty. I went down and signed the dotted line, and took an oath to serve my country.

I was to fly out from PDX two weeks later for boot camp in San Diego, California. I said my goodbyes to Nancy and my parents, then walked into the airport. Once I was inside, a recruiter placed me in a line with other recruits, and told us to stand at attention until everyone had arrived. We were then given a short speech and marched down to our boarding gate. As we marched, I could see the expression on the other recruits' faces, and wondered what these guys were thinking. Here we were, going to fight for our country, yet the looks we were getting were not supportive. People looked angry, and that made us feel bad about what we were doing.

Once on the plane, everyone was in good spirits, and looking forward to a new adventure. Little did we know that many of us would never return. We were laughing and getting to know each other, and talking about boot camp and what it would be like, and whether or not we could handle it. When we finally landed in San Diego, it was about 1:00 a.m., and I was pretty tired. We were put on a bus and driven out to the San Diego Naval Base, where we unloaded. There was a warm breeze blowing, and you could see the stars above. It was 2:00 a.m. when we were taken to a covered area, and they sat us down for another speech. When the first-class petty officer was done talking, he asked us who would like to volunteer. Who do you think raised his hand? The petty officer looked at me and said, "The first thing you should learn is never to volunteer." Then he indicated that I would be mopping the halls of the barracks until 5:00 a.m., while the others were sleeping. I never volunteered again. With very little sleep, the next morning came quickly. We were told to get dressed and assemble outside the barracks. We all knew it was the beginning of a new way of life for us.

Boot Camp San Diego
(MARCH 1969)

AFTER ASSEMBLING OUTSIDE THE BARRACKS, WE were marched across the grinder to the mess hall and told to get in line. After watching the cooks fry a thirty-second egg, I decided to have cereal and toast. The cooks were terrible, and didn't care if you liked the food or not. You would hear the command, "Move on!" every few seconds, but no one was asking for seconds. After breakfast, we assembled on the grinder, which is a large piece of blacktop or asphalt set aside to teach recruits how to march. From that moment on, we marched everywhere, every day, until we became one massive body that could turn on a dime and go completely in the opposite direction with one command, never losing a step.

That first morning we were introduced to Senior Chief Petty Officer Allison, who we found to be our new company commander. He didn't waste any time. He welcomed us to boot camp and assembled us into squads. He told us our squads would always assemble together in the same order. Then he told us that when all the squads were assembled, they would become one large body, which is called a company. The company was made up of forty men. The first person in each squad was the squad leader. He was in charge of the rest of the squad for roll call, and kept his squad members in step when marching. Looking at Senior Chief Allison, you would see a man about 165 pounds, who stood about five foot eight, with red hair and a wiry build. He commanded respect, and you had better show it or he was in your face, big time. I learned, very quickly, that there was no place for individuality. You were a part of a fighting unit, and all forty men were expected to think alike for a common goal. I was used to this type of team concept in football, so I fit right in. Some of the men were used to doing their own thing, and they had a tough time. There was always someone getting yelled at because they were saying or doing the wrong thing.

The first day we marched all day long. Our first stop was the building where you got all your hair cut off. I already knew how that felt. We all looked pretty funny with our new look. Then we went to the next building, where once again, we stood in line. We got issued our uniforms and a sea bag to put them in, along with our work clothes or dungarees. The sea bag was your new suitcase. It would go all over the world with you, and carry everything you owned. We continued to march for eight solid weeks, from one building to another.

One night when we were asleep in our barracks, the door flew open at about midnight, and all hell broke loose. Five senior petty officers came in, yelling, "Get out of those racks! This is a stand-tall inspection, and you have three minutes to make your space perfect." All the lessons I had learned in football helped me through that moment. I jumped up with forty other men, running around trying to make our racks (beds) up for inspection. When I was done, I stood in front of my space, at attention and ready for inspection. One of the petty officers came up and got in my face. For whatever reason I couldn't get a smile off my face. He started yelling at me, calling me names, telling me how stupid I looked with that smile on my face. He told me to drop down and give him fifty push-ups, which I did without hesitation. Then I got back up and stood at attention—and once more the smile returned. This really made the petty officer mad, so he went over and grabbed four pieces (rifles) and told me to hold out my arms, which I did. He placed the pieces in my arms, and told me to run up and down the barracks. Again, I did it without hesitation.

Finally, when he told me to stop, the other men couldn't believe what they saw—when I was back to attention, the smile returned. It just wouldn't leave. After the officer yelled at me some more, there was moment of silence. The petty officers looked at each other and said, "At ease." Then they went back into the barrack's office. We were all just standing there for a while, when one of the petty officers came out and told me to follow him, which I did without hesitation. When I got into the office, they shut the door and just looked at me as I stood at attention. There was no smile on my face now. After some time, one of the petty officers said, "You have been chosen to be the recruit company petty officer in charge of Company 220 in this barracks." Then they told me that there were expectations. I replied to each one with, "Yes, sir, Senior Chief Petty Officer." When we walked back into the barracks, all the men came to attention. The petty officer in charge announced to the men that I was the new company command petty officer, and to obey my orders or else. Then they said, "At ease!" and left as quickly as they had come.

For the next eight weeks I was in charge when Senior Chief Allison was not there. I believe at the end of the eight weeks the men had had enough of me. I pushed them hard, like my coaches had pushed me in football practice. I'm not sure, at the end of the eight weeks, whether the men liked me. But I believe they respected what I had done. Company 220 had won every award handed out in boot camp, and we were given the title "Honor Company." When we marched around the base, everyone knew we were the best, and the men were proud of that. Graduation day finally came, and it was a great honor. As we passed and were reviewed by our commanding officers, we were all excited. I thought I was on my way to becoming the next General Patton. We all received our orders. Mine said I was on my way to the *USS Mars*, a large combat supply ship that I would board in the Philippine Islands.

Welcome aboard the USS Mars AFS-1
(1969–70)

THE SAME DAY AS GRADUA-tion, we had our sea bags packed. When the barracks were empty, we boarded the bus to the San Diego airport. We had two weeks to see our families before reporting to our new duty stations.

After the two weeks at home, I was once again on a plane to McCord Air Force Base in California. This time I was in full uniform. I was a different man after boot camp, and ready for my new home aboard the *USS Mars*. The *Mars* was a combat supply ship that I was to meet up with at Subic Bay in the Philippine Islands. While I waited for the plane to take me there, I was pretty tired. I remember sitting down on a bench near the boarding gate to the big 747 that would fly us to Subic Bay. It was a calm morning, and once again I felt a gentle, warm breeze and the sunshine on my face.

It was hard for me to keep my eyes open and not doze off. Another sailor came and sat down on the bench with me. He had just bought a large new transistor radio inside the airport. He sat the radio down between us and pulled the antenna up, starting to listen to some music. After a short time I went back to dozing off. When I closed my eyes, all of sudden, without warning, I flinched—big time! Don't ask me why, but my hand flew out to catch myself from falling, and I karate-chopped his new radio's antenna, bending it in half.

I felt really bad, apologizing and telling him how sorry I was. You wouldn't believe the expression on this guy's face. He didn't say anything. After trying to straighten the antenna, he picked his radio up and walked away, shaking his head. I never forgot that moment, and never quite understood why I had flinched so hard. I must have been really tired.

Some more time passed, and finally we boarded the plane, and away we went. All I saw for hours was seawater and more seawater. Finally, the captain announced that we were coming into Subic Bay; shortly after, we landed.

It was the first time I had been out of the United States, and I didn't know what to expect. When we got off the plane, the air was humid and it smelled like a toilet; I mean, it was *bad*! I realized that I was now in a completely different world. We were quickly loaded onto a military bus—a school bus painted navy blue, with the windows covered in chicken wire. The bus driver announced that we were headed for the loading dock, and from there we would be taken out to our ship. I didn't understand the chicken wire over the windows until a rock slammed up against the side of the bus. The driver just kept driving, and didn't seem to be concerned. I couldn't believe the conditions in which these people lived. Their homes were nothing more than little pieced-together shacks. As we drove by, you could see them staring at us with sad eyes. I couldn't help but be thankful and proud that I was an American.

As we continued, the roads were rough, and the bus felt like it would fall apart from all the potholes. When we pulled up to the loading dock, we were told where to wait, and that a launch (boat) would pick us up and take us to the *Mars*. While waiting, some sailors who had been in town gathered around us. I assumed these guys would be some of my new shipmates. I could smell the alcohol from a distance and watched them as they stumbled around, trying not to fall over. They were dead drunk! When the boat arrived, one of the sailors fell right in from the dock, and just lay there, passed out. I was not impressed.

As we headed out toward the *Mars*, I could see it in the distance. It was a huge—an awesome sight, sitting there and waiting for its next adventure in Vietnam. Our launch pulled up alongside, and we walked up the gangway, saluting the officer on duty. I was amazed at the amount of steel, feeling the hard deck below my feet. The chief petty officer on duty said, "Welcome aboard the *Mars*. I'll show you to your quarters so you can get some sleep."

Life aboard Mars
(1969-70)

THE NEXT MORNING, MY LIFE ABOARD *MARS* STARTED at 6:00 a.m. A whistle came over the loudspeaker, followed by a voice that said, "Now reveille. Now reveille. All hands on deck. Now reveille." All of a sudden, sailors were flying out of their racks, getting ready to stand inspection on deck. Like everyone else, I hustled not to be late. Once on deck, we were shown where to go, and how to stand inspection. The routine would be the same for the next eighteen months. You stood inspection with a clean-shaven face and a neatly pressed uniform, and answered, "Yes, sir" or "No, sir" if asked a question.

After inspection, we returned to the main deck to meet our new captain. As we arrived, we were all individually approached by him with a salute. "Welcome aboard", he said; asking us each where we were from. When he was done, he stood back and the petty officer on deck announced, "The captain is on the deck." We all popped to attention and saluted the captain; then he was gone. At that point, we were told to relax, as some of the chief petty officers had arrived to assign our duty stations.

When my test scores were reviewed, the officers looked at me and told me I would be going to the communications department as a signalman striker. I guess my scores had gone up after being re-tested in boot camp. That saved me from being a deckhand. They also took another seaman next to me, by the name of James Bennett. I didn't know it at the time, but James and I would become good friends. Jim was about five foot ten, with reddish-blond hair and freckles. He looked strong as a bull. I found out later that he was a great baseball talent who would never be discovered.

A few minutes later, James and I found ourselves at the top of the ship, on the signal deck. We were at the very top of the ship, and you could see the other men working below, keeping the *Mars* shipshape. The chief petty officer asked us to step into the signal shack, which was a small, grey building, eight feet wide and at least twelve feet long. When we entered, we were surrounded by the other signalman, and introduced one at a time.

Chase was the chief petty officer who had brought us up to the signal deck. He was big, overweight, and missing some teeth. I decided later that he was one of the most obnoxious people I had ever met in my life. The other chief petty officer was James Hardin, who wasn't much better. At least he had all his teeth and you could talk to him. James was tall, medium-built, and always telling dirty jokes—whether you wanted to hear them or not.

Then there was Willis, who was a petty officer second-class and a darned nice guy, but had a stuttering problem. Sometimes, it would take him five minutes to say just one word. Why he was in communications, I have no clue! In a serious situation, when you needed a quick response, Willis would try to speak so hard that his eyeballs would roll back in his head, and he would look like he was about to pass out.

One of the third-class signalmen was Bryce—who was, without a doubt, just a great guy. He never got upset about anything, and would always laugh at your dumb jokes. Bryce did his job and did it well—always with a smile.

For the next few months I worked hard at becoming a signalman. One ritual I enjoyed was the rough weather. I would go out on a platform that was attached to the side of the ship, where there was a huge searchlight. This searchlight was used to signal other ships from miles away. During a storm, when the ship would take significant rolls from side to side. I would sit on the edge of the platform and let my feet dangle over the water. When the ship took a big roll, it felt like I could almost touch the water with my feet. It was like a carnival ride; great fun! At that time, I was young, and had no fear, whatsoever.

A signalman's job was to communicate with other ships and sea ports along the coast, as well as aircraft flying overhead. Communication was done by flashing light, signal flags, or Morse code. At other times we would use a method of flying flags or stringing flags from our mast to let everyone know our intentions and who we were. We were not only a supply vessel, but had the ability to engage in combat if necessary. For example, if we signaled an aircraft or ship and they didn't respond in the proper fashion, then we would shoot across their bow. If they refused to communicate they would get fired upon. We were never under attack by sea or by air, which was good because the life expectancy of a signalman under attack was thirty seconds, because you were on the top of the ship.

As time went on, I was assigned to the fifty-caliber machine gun on the starboard side of the ship during general quarters—i.e., whenever there was an emergency situation, such as an attack or a collision with another ship. It was a big gun, mounted to the railing, and I stood on a platform when shooting it. It was hard to hit the target, because when you fired, it would jump around a lot. We were taught to aim low and walk up on the target and then hit it as you went by. Knowing how this gun worked was important and we were trained to disassemble it blindfolded. I can remember when we were in Da Nang harbor and we went to general quarters. I jumped on the fifty-caliber machine gun. There was activity on the shoreline and US aircraft were making scraping runs and being fired upon. Captain gave the order and I opened up with the fifty. The deck was wet, and as I was shooting, I slipped on the platform. The gun swirled around and I almost took the captain's head off. It's a little funny now, but nobody thought it was funny back then.

Every few months or so we would change duties at general quarters. After I had served my time with the fifty, I was assigned to the helo deck, which was at the aft part of the ship, where the helicopters landed. For the next few months, when we went to general quarters, I would report to the helo deck, where I would put on a fire resistant suit. My job was to pull people to safety if one of our helicopters caught fire. If that happened, I was supposed to climb on board, find the pilots and help them get out. I seem to remember one of our jolly green giants coming in on fire and hitting the deck. It started to slip over the side. I headed for it, and just as I was about to jump on board, it went over the side. Someone grabbed me and pulled me back to safety. This story seems so real to me but I can't remember where it came from. I've come to realize it must have been a terrifying recurring dream I had while on board the *Mars*, performing this duty in a stressful situation.

After my few months ended at the helo deck I moved on to sea rescue, or "man overboard" duty. My new job at general quarters was to help rescue men who ended up in the water and needed help. The frightening realization was that men didn't end up in the water unless the ship was under attack or there was a bad storm. I would jump in a lifeboat with a flare gun, paddle out in rough seas, and try to find the people who had fallen overboard. I remember being in the lifeboat during a drill, going after a fake body in the water. The lifeboat rolled and pitched so much, that when I shot my flare gun, the flare went toward the captain, who was standing on the bridge, watching the drill. I thought I could hear him cussing and yelling, "Who is that guy?"

My last assignment—the one all sailors must serve before spending every minute training to be a signalman—was on the ship's mess decks, or galley. Everyone on board serves six weeks in the kitchen. I didn't want to cook, so I ran the automatic dishwasher. I guess my biggest moment washing dishes came when the dishwasher suddenly stopped. I couldn't figure out what the problem was, so I decided to remove the dish rack and crawl inside with a big crescent wrench in my hand. Once inside, I started beating on a few parts—the darned thing started with me inside! I had water shooting at me from all sides. I backed out in a New York minute, but was completely soaked with water and soap from hell to breakfast. Well, guess what? That night, in my rack, I relived the whole event in my sleep. I got up on all fours, backed out the rear of my rack, right over the top of another sailor. I ended up sticking my foot in a fan that was at the end of his rack. It caused quite a commotion in the sleeping quarters. The crew laughed about it for days, and I had to visit sick bay to get my foot bandaged up. Six weeks passed, and I was once again on top of the ship, learning my new job. Days passed, and one day became many. I tried to do the best job I could, stopping now and then to think about home.

The Big Mistake
(1970)

ONE DAY, COMING INTO PORT IN TAIWAN, I WAS OR-
dered to show our entrance into port by stringing a wire cable from the mast to the front of the ship. Then I was supposed to fly different flags which would announce our ship's call sign, or its name, to let everyone know who we were. As I was standing on a platform at the bow of the ship, hooking up the wire cable to string the flags, the wire cable suddenly got caught in the wind-less—the motor that releases and pulls up the anchor. Seeing the wire caught, I grabbed it and tried to pull it out. I can still hear the cable tightening down, and then the sound of it snapping. I don't remember anything after that, except lying on the deck and then trying to get up. It was a bad idea to grab that cable. I had been knocked down to the deck below from the platform above. Two or three men grabbed me. They laid me back down on the deck and applied pressure to my forehead and chin to stop the bleeding. A few moments later a stretcher arrived, and I was hauled off to sick bay. As I lay on the operating table I was very upset that I had been so stupid as to let this happen. They told me later that I was so mad that I took a swing at one of them. I received sixty stitches to my chin, lip, and forehead. To say the least, I was a mess. After they were done stitching me up, they put me in a small room for observation. When I was there for a while, I finally got up off of the bed and looked at my face in the mirror. I didn't recognize myself anymore. All I could see was something ugly. And then I realized I would never look the same again. At that moment, my

life changed. My face looked deformed. I knew I couldn't face Nancy or my family looking like this.

In the days and months that followed, people stared at me as I walked around the ship, like I was some kind of deformed creature. I stopped writing home. My performance on the ship went down. I was depressed. I felt this accident would haunt me for the rest of my life.

As time passed and I healed, I received a letter from Nancy saying she had met someone else, and was engaged to be married. She had met a marine captain in Europe. He was much older than she was, and I think she was impressed by his position and wealth. Nancy was like that—always impressed by someone older or in charge. There was nothing I could do, especially looking like I did. Besides, I was different now. I had lost a lot of confidence.

Things couldn't get much worse. One day, we were off the coast of Vietnam and a song came over the ship's loudspeaker. We all looked at each other; we couldn't figure out why they were playing, "I Left My Heart in San Francisco." A few moments later, the captain's voice came over the loudspeaker; he announced that we were headed home. We would be in the San Francisco dry dock for six months for repairs. We all just looked at each other. Then cheers went up—we were all pretty excited. The ship started making a slow turn towards home, once again playing the song.

At that moment, I just happened to be walking by the captain's quarters. He stopped me and asked how I was doing. We talked for a while, and it came up that when I was discharged I wanted to attend Linfield College back home, and play football for the Linfield Wildcats. He looked at me and listened. After a brief moment, he went to his desk, pulled out a form and put my name on it, and signed it. Then I signed it. The form was a "Reduction in Force Order," which meant he was letting me out early. With a smile, he told me that in four weeks I would be home. Then he said, "Good luck in college."

I couldn't believe it! After shaking my hand, he went on his way. I've never forgotten that moment. It was the start of my return.

Heading Home
(DECEMBER 1970)

Before heading to San Francisco, we made a short two-week stop in Yakoska, Japan, for some R&R. Most of the crew went to Tokyo to purchase stereo equipment because it was so cheap and it would be our last chance. Some of the crew bought motorcycles to take back. Because the *Mars* was a combat supply ship we had plenty of room to store our personal items to take back to the States.

I recall one morning, standing at the railing of the signal bridge, looking down at the dock. I noticed a sailor had purchased a new motorcycle and had just taken it out of the shipping container and was starting to assemble it on the dock. I watched how hard he worked most of the day, putting his new ride together. Standing there, and watching him, I imagined how great it was going to be when he boarded his new crotch-rocket and rode off down the pier. After many hours, he finally finished. He stood back and looked at what he had worked so hard to accomplish. It was shiny and beautiful—an awesome sight. He put some gas in it and put his helmet on. He started it up and revved the motor a few times. Then he drove right smack into the side of the cement warehouse, destroying the front of the bike.

I couldn't help but duck down out of sight, and couldn't hold back my laughter as I heard all the cussing and yelling for the next ten minutes. I've never forgotten that day—and I still can't help but laugh, even though the guy got a bad deal after such hard work.

When we left Japan, we stopped in Hawaii for a week, for more R&R. While in Hawaii, I talked to the ship's doctor, who had stitched me up. I asked if he could operate on my chin to help me look more like me. After a long discussion he told me he couldn't promise it would look any better, but he was willing to try to remove some of the unsightly scar tissue.

After some time on the operating table and a bold attempt to cut away scar tissue, I looked much better. My chin looked halfway normal, and even though the scar was still there, it was now in the crease of my chin. I was thankful for the improvement. Even though my chin looked better, I already had signs of PTSD from the trauma. I would look and obsess over my chin every day. I was no longer fearless. I was still very angry inside. I believed people continued to stare at me. I never really understood why the scar on my chin had such an impact on me until years later. I knew I never wanted to make a mistake like the one I made on the ship that day.

Homecoming

WE FINISHED UP R&R IN HAWAII AND HEADED FOR San Francisco. I was released from active service a few days after we arrived, and put on a plane flight home. Because of my accident, I hadn't written home for months, and like I indicated, Nancy had gone south.

When I arrived at the Portland airport, there was no one there to greet me or say thanks for serving your country. There was just a bunch of protesters who tried to make me feel bad about my uniform and Vietnam. I went to the front of the airport and caught a Greyhound bus out to Beaverton, to where my parents had moved after leaving Washington State. When I knocked on the front door, they couldn't believe it was me. I talked with them awhile, told them about my new scar and that I had been let out early. I then brought up college and told them I was going back and I wanted to play football and be the first in our family to have a college degree. My parents were supportive, but also said they had little money to help me. I was both excited for the future and glad to be home and ready to move on.

A few days later, I borrowed my dad's car and drove down to McMinnville, Oregon, to Linfield College. I was pretty excited when I walked into the athletic office and met "Mama Cat." She turned out to be Coach Rutschman's wife—"Mama" to all his players, and an all-around great lady. She smiled, then asked how she could help. I asked if I could talk to Coach Rutschman. A few minutes later, when I entered Rutschman's office, he immediately remembered who I was, that I had played for Sunset High School, and that I had played nose guard for Mouse Davis. He was happy to see me. I told him I needed his help to come to Linfield and play football. We talked about me "walking on"—if I did well, there would be an athletic grant available to me. He also indicated I would have to attend a junior college to bring up my grades. I realized it wouldn't be easy, but I was determined not to fail this time, and to give it my all. I left his office excited that I might get to play football again, while attending a great institution like Linfield.

After settling in at home and going over my plan with my parents, I enrolled in Portland Community College and took the courses I needed to attend Linfield. After two terms of hard work and finally getting some good grades, I applied at Linfield and was accepted. I was ready to "walk on" at Linfield—claiming my college degree and my defensive position with the Wildcats.

CHAPTER SEVEN
COLLEGE YEARS

Heading to Linfield
(FALL 1971)

BEFORE I WENT DOWN TO LINFIELD I PLANNED
to search through the papers, to purchase a Triumph sports car. The
car was part of the dream I had envisioned for going to college.
During my active duty overseas I had saved over two thousand dollars, and had brought it home with me to buy a Triumph sports car. I
had also saved money to buy some nice stereo equipment that I had
already purchased and brought home from Japan. I had done this
while watching my shipmates spend their money getting drunk, while
I was putting my money away for another day. That day had arrived.

One morning I read about this 1969 TR-6 Triumph owned by a
doctor who was selling it for two thousand dollars. It was in show-
room condition. My dad and I jumped in his car and went to see

it. When we arrived, we met the doctor and made our way to his garage. When we opened the garage door, there sat the TR-6 under a nice cover. When the doctor pulled the cover off, I couldn't believe what I was looking at. The car looked like it was brand-new! It was a deep burgundy, with a black convertible top. There wasn't a scratch or mark or blemish anywhere. This was a perfect car—so clean you could eat off the floor. The interior had black leather seats that smelled brand-new and were in perfect condition. The beautiful walnut dash was finished to perfection, with an array of sporty gauges for fuel, temperature, and speed. The doctor had really taken excellent care of this speedster.

Well, there wasn't a lot of negotiation. I looked for a few moments, then turned to the doctor and said, "I'll take it!" My dad and the doctor looked at each other with surprise. The doctor said, "Wouldn't you like to drive it first?" I said, "I will—on my way home." I handed him two thousand dollars and then watched as he signed over the title to me. I got in the TR-6, backed her out of the garage, said "thank you" to the doctor, and headed home with a big smile and my dad following me. I never looked back. The car drove perfect, just like I knew it would. I had just fulfilled one of my dreams!

Getting Ready for Football
(1971)

Because I was not going to let my Linfield dream pass me by, my workouts for football were routine and tough. I was working at a health club and used the weight room every day to get stronger. I received summer letters from Linfield and learned what was going to be expected of me when I arrived in the fall. At that time, Coach Rutschman asked his players to be in great shape by running ten 240-yard, timed sprints. Each sprint needed to be under thirty-five seconds, with just one minute rest between sprints. When I arrived, not only could I run ten of these sprints—I had mastered twenty-two, all in under thirty-five seconds.

To illustrate how important this football opportunity was to me, when I arrived at Linfield that first night, I couldn't sleep. So when everyone else was sound asleep, I went out to the football field, with a flashlight and stopwatch, and ran the ten 240s under time in the moonlight. At 8:00 a.m. the next morning, I did it all over again at the first practice with the football team. I was strong, fast, and ready to be a Wildcat.

When football started it only took three days to become the starting nose guard for Linfield. I went 100 percent every day in every practice. I felt the coaches were happy with my performance and they could see my desire to play.

About a week into practices, we were running sprints when I fell and hurt my shoulder. Even though my shoulder hurt I kept going hard in practice until Coach Rutschman called me over and asked why I was favoring my right side. I told him I had fallen during sprints and hurt my shoulder. Long story short, he told me to have a doctor check it out. When I saw the doctor, he gave me some bad news: I had a broken collarbone and couldn't play for six weeks. Even though I was disappointed, I kept doing what I could to stay in shape. Six weeks later I was once again ready to go, excited to play in my first game as a Wildcat football player.

I can remember the team loading out front of the stadium on the track where the bus was waiting. I went to step on the bus to play at Pacific University in Forest Grove, Oregon, and at that moment, Coach Rutschman said he needed to talk with me. He told me that Pacific had just called and indicated that I was half a credit short, and not eligible to play this season. I couldn't believe Pacific University would take the time to check my transcripts. You can't imagine the disappointment I felt after all the hard work I had done to get ready. Coach Rutschman told me he would honor my athletic grant and work-study, and he would redshirt me for the 1971 season. So I continued to attend Linfield for the rest of 1971.

During the school year I went on to meet some great people, and after many hours of talking with friends and professors, I decided I would become a teacher and coach after graduating from Linfield. This was an important decision which gave me the direction I needed to be successful and to help others. I had just made it through my first year at Linfield and had still not lost my dream of being a Wildcat football player. Because of Ad Rutschman and Linfield College I was on my way to helping thousands of young people over a thirty-year career in education and coaching.

Back on the Field
(1972)

IN 1972 I WORKED EVEN HARDER TO GET READY FOR fall and making the team once again. When I reported to Linfield that next fall I was hell-bent on being the starting nose guard. Even though my accident on board the USS *Mars* was having an effect on me and my relationships with others, I worked hard on the football field and found the distraction helpful. I had a good first two weeks, and once again I was the starting nose guard.

On September 16th, the Wildcats traveled to Central Washington University. That was a special day for me. It was my first football game since 1968. Not only was I back—I was back big time. After watching game film against Central Washington I made sixteen unassisted tackles with an additional eight assisted tackles, for a total of twenty-four tackles in a single game. According to the records, that was and still is the most tackles in a single game in the history of Linfield football. The following Monday, I was praised by the coaches and picked "Top Cat of the Week," and interviewed by the *Oregonian*. Without a doubt, it was the best game I ever played.

Our next game was September 23, against the Portland State Vikings, at Linfield. Both Central Washington and Portland State were in a higher division, and both were favored to beat us. Once again I played well, and had a total of sixteen tackles in the mud, along with at least two fumble recoveries. We lost 6-0, but the team played well and I was having a lot of fun. In game three against Pacific University on September 30, I was hit hard in the upper right leg and didn't see action in the fourth quarter. Even though I didn't play that fourth quarter, I still managed to rack up four unassisted tackles, four assisted tackles, two quarterback sacks, two forced fumbles, and two fumble recoveries. I was still hell-bent for leather, and playing hard and knocking people around. I was healthy and playing well. The hit to my right leg would put me on the bench against Whitman College on October 7, and I would return against Willamette on October 14.

Even though my leg wasn't one hundred percent, I acted like it was, so I could play. I never was good at standing and watching. I needed to be in the game. On October 14, against Willamette University, I was able to make eight tackles, two quarterback sacks, one quarterback hurry, and one forced fumble. My leg held up, but it wasn't quite there yet, and being out the past week had made me tired. The next week in practice, my leg was acting up, so I didn't practice all week, and didn't play against the College of Idaho on October 21. I was disappointed, and could feel myself getting weaker and weaker as I missed practice. I knew that to play my best football, I needed to be at full strength. I couldn't run, and I couldn't lift weights with that bad leg.

Our next game was on October 28, against Lewis & Clark College. I suited up, but played less than half the game. I seemed a step slower and somewhat weaker. I managed four tackles, one forced fumble, and one quarterback hurry. I wasn't upset, but I knew why my playing ability had been diminished. I was not in the physical shape I needed to be in to compete, and it was showing.

Our next game wouldn't be until November 11, against Pacific Lutheran University, which was always our strongest rival. I thought I would have some time to heal and gain some strength back. But it just wasn't meant to be.

That next week I was very sick, with a bad virus. My anxiety was acting up, and I was having panic attacks—not knowing why they were happening. It scared me a lot. I was sick as a dog for almost two weeks with fever chills. I needed to get better and get back on the field. I went to see the doctor. He put me on penicillin, which I immediately had an allergic reaction to—and that brought my panic attacks to a new level. Sometimes I didn't feel I could breathe, and my stomach was always upset. I would sit in class at Linfield and need to get up and leave. I was scared, and I couldn't figure out why I would get so obsessed with my physical condition. I got to a point where the virus was gone, but the after-effects of my anxiety remained. And there was something more that I didn't understand that was going on with me, and it wasn't going away.

When I returned to practice, I was weak, and not the same. The defensive coach thought I was being lazy, so he sent me over to the ropes to run by myself, and to make me feel bad. Coach Rutschman saw me. He called me over and asked what I was doing at the ropes. I told him what had happened, and he told me to go back with the team. It never came up again, and the defensive coach had a different attitude the next day. I believe Coach Rutschman knew I was not quite myself, and he also knew I was not lazy.

On November 11, 1972, we played Pacific Lutheran University. I suited up, and only played a small amount of time in the first quarter. I think it was payback by the defensive coach. I came to realize he was a kind of a jerk, and probably thought I got him in trouble with Coach Rutschman, so he wouldn't play me. He was the first coach in football at

Linfield I didn't care for, and the only person at Linfield who I felt didn't belong there. I guess he didn't know me or my love of football very well.

Next, we were scheduled to play the University of Hawaii. This was to be our final game. I didn't think I would be picked to go, but I was doing better in practice and made the traveling squad. I was still on medication when we arrived in Hawaii and suited up for our first practice. During the practice, I started to feel real funny. My stomach just wouldn't settle down. Believe it or not, I walked up to Coach Rutschman and told him that my stomach was really upset. I asked if I could borrow a dollar to go across the street to McDonald's and get a milkshake. He gave me a pretty funny look, then pulled out a dollar and handed it to me. I hustled across the street and stood in line with full practice gear on, ordering a vanilla milkshake, in Hawaii. When I returned to the field, I had downed the shake and once again started to practice. Five minutes later, I was on the sideline, lying on the bench, shaking, with my face red and flushed. The coaches decided to rush me to the hospital and have me checked out. I was stuffed in the back of a rental car and rushed downtown. When we pulled up outside the emergency room, they decided to lay me down on a park bench outside the hospital and have the doctor check me out there. He looked at me, checked a few things, and then asked, "Are you on any medication?" I nodded. Then he asked me to try and calm down and just relax, and told me he thought I was having a panic attack.

So as he spoke with me, I started to calm down and started feeling better. He thought that I had taken the medication too long, and it had killed all the bacteria in my system, and when I started feeling bad it set off the panic attack. The first thing he told me to do was not to take any more medication, and to eat plenty of cottage cheese and yogurt to replenish the bacteria in my body. By the time he was done talking, I had calmed down. I sat up, and a little while later got back in the car and headed for the hotel. The next few days,

I felt a lot of anxiety, being so far away from home. But I got through practice and made it to game night.

Hawaii was also a division higher than Linfield, and was picked to win. Even though we had won our league championship, we were no match for the Islanders. I played, but was not very effective. I was glad when the game was over. After the game, we headed for the airport and boarded the plane. I had a seat all to myself and slept the whole flight. I was happy that we were back home, and that I had finished my first full season as a Linfield Wildcat. I attended classes the rest of the year—looking forward to the next football season and a chance to heal up and get stronger again.

Faith

ONE OF THE GREAT PROGRAMS ON CAMPUS DURING my time at Linfield was the Fellowship of Christian Athletes. Time and time again I would observe these athletes, and their actions and friendships on campus. It appeared to me that their faith was in every aspect of their life, but especially on the football field. I found myself drawn to and inspired by these individuals and their belief in God.

Becoming a Christian Athlete changed my whole perspective on why I was playing football. It gave me a renewed spirit and direction. I wanted to play football for the right reasons—I wanted to play for God, my parents, and my community. At that time, I loved what was good in the world—not what other people thought was good, but truths that came from years and years of trial and error. Truths that were as true as they had been hundreds of years before. When I read the Bible I tried to pull as many of these truths out of my reading as I could, so I could implement them into my life.

One Sunday during the football season, I was in church, sitting with a group of friends, listening to the pastor's stories about faith and inspiration. All of a sudden, he turned and looked right at me. He started talking about how he had attended Linfield's football game the day before. Then, out of the blue, he started talking about how this one player on Linfield's team was so inspiring to him—how he loved his effort and enthusiasm on the field. As the pastor spoke, he was animated and fired up. He then indicated that this player was here in the church today, sitting in the congregation. He went on to say what a pleasure it was, having nose guard Larry Geigle attending, and how much fun it had been to watch him on the football field. After that, he went on with the rest of his sermon.

I will never forget that day in church; it was better than any football victory. Today, I feel the same about my faith in God. I love the true lessons of life and know there is no way anyone can live up to all of them. That doesn't mean we stop trying. I've seen what is good and right in this world, and it comes from doing the right thing.

I really believed back then that people lived their lives through example, not empty words. I found wonderful examples of great people at Linfield on and off the field. The great ones didn't talk much, but spoke loudly with their actions around campus and on the football field. For example, when they would help an opposing player up off the ground after knocking the whoop-tee-do out of them.

On purpose, I have not talked about the impact of my accident on the *USS Mars*, and the effects it had on me during my college days. Even though PTSD was present at Linfield, I never really understood how it affected my performance and consistency. This was the 70s, and PTSD was not fully understood or even acknowledged. You were supposed to "suck it up" and be tough. But it's a strange condition. I have paid a dear price for an accident that happened to me at the age of nineteen. Looking back, years later, at my days at Linfield, I can truly say that accident on the *USS Mars* had a dramatic influence on my college performance, and my ability to trust, feel safe, and be secure. Not only was the trauma still present, but it continued to expand its influence in my life. It would do so forever.

Linfield
(FALL 1973)

The summer before my third year at Linfield College, I had stayed during the summer months, taking classes so I could graduate early. That cut my time in college down to three years. Nineteen seventy three would be my final season. Once again I had worked hard to get ready to be a Wildcat. My faith and confidence had grown. I was rested, physically healthy, and strong as a bull.

During the summer of 1973, I was at Linfield, enjoying the hot days and warm nights. I had acquired my tan, and wore cut-offs and T-shirts. One day I ran into a girl I really liked. Ellen was beautiful, with freckles and light-brown hair that went all the way down to her waist. She had become a great friend to me while at Linfield. Ellen had spent her last semester studying in Germany, so we hadn't seen each other in a long time. We got to talking, and decided to go camping up in the Mt. Jefferson wilderness area—near Bend, Oregon.

Before classes started that fall, we packed up her car and headed toward our camping adventure. The Mt. Jefferson area was beautiful forestland, untouched by man. The old growth trees were spectacular.

We hiked in about five miles and set up our little camp. I was doing okay until some campers came by from the camp up above us. They told us to make sure our food was safe because bears had come through their camp the night before, looking for snacks. Well, my whole idea of camping fun went right out the window with the fear of being attacked and eaten by a bear. The bear news didn't seem to bother Ellen in the least.

Because it was summer and very warm, we really didn't think we needed a tent. We decided sleeping under the stars would be great fun. Of course, now that we were going to get eaten by bears, I wasn't very happy under the stars. I tried to be strong, so Ellen wouldn't notice I was a wimp. I wore a smile as much as I could.

Toward evening, we crawled into our sleeping bags, talking awhile. Soon it was very dark. I mean it was so dark I couldn't see an inch in front of my face. A bear could have been standing over me that very moment, and I wouldn't have been able to see him. I lay awake the entire night so I wouldn't get eaten alive. Ellen slept like a baby, though—she never woke up once. The next morning she bounced up, looking her beautiful self. As for me: I looked like you-know-what! I got up and tried to go into the lake to wash my face. But the water was so cold I started shaking. I had to get out and sit by the fire.

Thank God we only stayed one night. I was never so happy as when we got out of bear country and back into the car. I told Ellen she could drive home so I could take a short nap. I slept the whole way back. She probably wondered why I was so tired.

Ellen and I dated for a short period, and really liked each other until my past had its effect on our relationship. At that time, I couldn't understand my lack of trust in people, or where my fears were coming from. A few months later, Ellen and I parted ways. We never really spoke again. During our short relationship we had visited with Doctor Baffus at Linfield about my lack of trust. He indicated that without trust, our relationship was doomed to fail. He was right!

Back on the Field
(1973)

RIGHT AFTER I HAD GONE CAMPING WITH ELLEN, summer was over and it was time to play football. I was happy to be back on the field. I quickly won the starting nose guard position, and after a few weeks of practice, we were ready for our first game against Portland State on September 22, at the Civic Stadium in Portland. It was raining, and their field had the new artificial grass—although at the time it looked more like living-room carpet than grass. We had Portland State's number that year, and won 19-3. Coach Rutschman was pretty happy with our performance. I walked away with ten tackles and one forced fumble.

The following week, on September 29, we won against Whitworth College. I was flying high with fifteen tackles and another fumble recovery. I picked up a fumbled ball and ran fifteen yards before getting tackled. The next week, on October 6, we beat Willamette University at Linfield. I blocked a punt, forced a fumble, and made three tackles. The fourth game into the season was played on October 13, against the College of Idaho. I turned in thirteen tackles and another forced fumble.

Playing nose guard in college at 190 pounds dripping wet can get a little rough. The next week, against Lewis & Clark, I was coming down the field on a kickoff, and slammed my right hand into the helmet of an opposing player. This broke my hand, but I didn't know it at the time. It made me pretty mad. The very next play, when the ball was hiked, I gave a forearm to the center—and once again, I was in pain. When I was off the field, the team doctor grabbed me and had a look at my hand. He told me I was done playing—it appeared that my hand was broken in three places. He also said that if I went back in the game he would have to operate to wire my hand back together. I was done for the season—and since it was my last year at Linfield, I was done playing football. We lost that game to Lewis & Clark, 7-4. Coach Rutschman let us know how unhappy he was on the way back to Linfield.

The next four weeks went by pretty slowly, but finally the season was over. Once again we were league champions of our conference.

After all the league selections were announced and I didn't receive any honors, I stopped by Coach Rutschman's office and asked him if I had received any votes for all-league. He thought for a moment, and then said, "I think you got one vote." I was disappointed that for all my hard work I had only received one vote. I thought later that maybe I tried too hard, wearing myself down until I became injured and even sick. If I had stayed healthy and not missed so many games I would have received the votes and recognition I deserved.

I said goodbye to Linfield football, focusing on graduation in the spring and becoming a certified teacher.

My First Wife
(1973–1989)

A FEW MONTHS AFTER THE 1973 FOOTBALL SEASON was over, my friend Verjean called me, asking me to stop by her work and say hello. Verjean had been best friends with Nancy, my old girlfriend in high school. We had all grown up together.

I went over to where Verjean worked. As I was standing out front, a friend of hers walked by. Verjean stopped her, introducing her as "Debbie." Debbie was about five foot six—a cute blond with a wonderful smile and demeanor. We all talked awhile. Then we said our goodbyes and I went on my way. Later that day I received a phone call from my friend, who said, "Debbie would like you to go to a party with her, and she would like you to call her." Little did I know that Verjean had told Debbie that I would like her to go to a party with me, and that I would call her. It was the classic set-up, and we both fell for it big time.

So the party was on, and from the time I picked Debbie up we had a great time. Debbie was great fun, and liked to laugh a lot. You could tell she was a very smart girl. I was amazed at how well-read she was. We became very comfortable with each other during the party and started dating. One date led to another, and before you knew it, I was driving to her house to meet her mother and father. Back in the 70s, we all dressed a little funny. Thinking back now, I realize I looked ridiculous pulling up to her house. I had on a yellow, burgundy, and ruby-colored shirt; brown fake-leather pants; and bright-orange tennis shoes. My car was a blue 1969 Buick Wildcat, which was huge, like a battleship. It leaked water from the windshield onto my crotch every time it rained. I had to drive this thing around with a towel on my lap so it wouldn't look like I had wet my pants!

I wonder what Debbie's parents thought. Oh yeah, I forgot! Her Dad was the head of IBM for Portland, Oregon. Anyway, I walked into their living room and the whole family was sitting on the couch, waiting to size me up. Debbie's parents were well-to-do, and had a nice home. It didn't take long before I found them to be great people. Her dad was smart and a kick in the pants; always telling a funny joke. Her mother was the best cook, along with being well-dressed and excellent at keeping the house running smoothly. I quickly realized that Debbie had obtained a lot of her Dad's qualities, and her mother's ability to look nice. So for the next year we all got to know each other. I felt like I was part of the family.

Graduation from Linfield
(1974)

MY FINAL CLASS AT LINFIELD WAS STUDENT TEACHing. This is where the college would place you in an educational setting to give you a teaching experience. This experience would help you understand the everyday job of an educator.

My old high school football coach had moved to Hillsboro High School so I thought it would be great to do my student teaching with him. He accepted my application to be my advisor and show me the ropes. When I got to Hillsboro, I quickly learned that they had just won the high school 5A State Football Championship. Everyone at the school was pretty excited, including my old coach, Mouse Davis. After all his years of putting teams on the field, I couldn't think of anyone who deserved it more.

After spending the next twelve weeks under Coach Davis's watchful eyes, and teaching a number of different PE units, I was called into the office and told that Hillsboro School District liked what I had done in the classroom, and would like to interview me for a teaching position in PE. After meeting with them and going through the Hillsboro interview, I was not hired, so I went home. A few hours later that same day, my phone rang. It was Beaverton School District, wanting to interview me at Highland Park Middle School. They said they wanted to interview me at once. I think what happened is that Hillsboro had decided to hire another Linfield alumni, who had graduated from Hillsboro School District. They then called Beaverton and told them how much they liked me, and that's when I got the call for my interview at Highland Park.

On the day of the new interview I can still remember driving up to Highland Park Junior High, where the interview was going to take place. I was nervous, but optimistic and positive—an attitude that carried into the interview. The thing was, I was a very clean-cut young man, and I loved helping kids, and they could see that. They could see that once I was experienced, I would become a great mentor for students in my teaching and coaching. When the interview was over, I left with a good feeling, knowing I had done well.

I went home to my one-room boarding house, thinking how great it would be to be a teacher and coach at Highland Park. The next day I received a phone call and was offered the job. I accepted. Both excitement and fear set in. After settling down, I immediately jumped in my old leaky 1969 Buick Wildcat Battleship and drove down to Portland Volkswagen, where I traded that heap in for a brand-new bright-yellow VW Beetle. Back at Linfield I had needed money for school, so I sold the TR6 and bought the Wildcat—so it was nice to be back in a new-smelling car. My car payment was $50 a month, and my starting salary for teaching was a huge $575 a month! I was rich! After my car payment I still had $525 left.

After buying the car I decided to look for a one-bedroom apartment close to my new job. I found one and immediately moved in. I was on cloud nine. I thought to myself how proud I was, and all I had accomplished in the last four years.

The scar on my face was looking better and didn't stand out quite as much. I thought about the doctor on the USS Mars who had really done an outstanding job when he operated the second time. I didn't talk about it earlier, but when I came home from the Navy, my chin was flaring up. I developed a staph infection that scared me and added to my trauma issues. I had gone to the doctor—he had put me on large doses of penicillin, and still the staph infection didn't seem to want to leave. After a while, he told me that was all the penicillin he could give me—hopefully there was enough in my system to kill the infection. Lucky for me, the infection finally left, and my chin healed up. But because I had taken so much penicillin, I think it set me up for the reaction I had at college. Too much penicillin had produced an allergic reaction, as well as the panic attack in Hawaii during football practice.

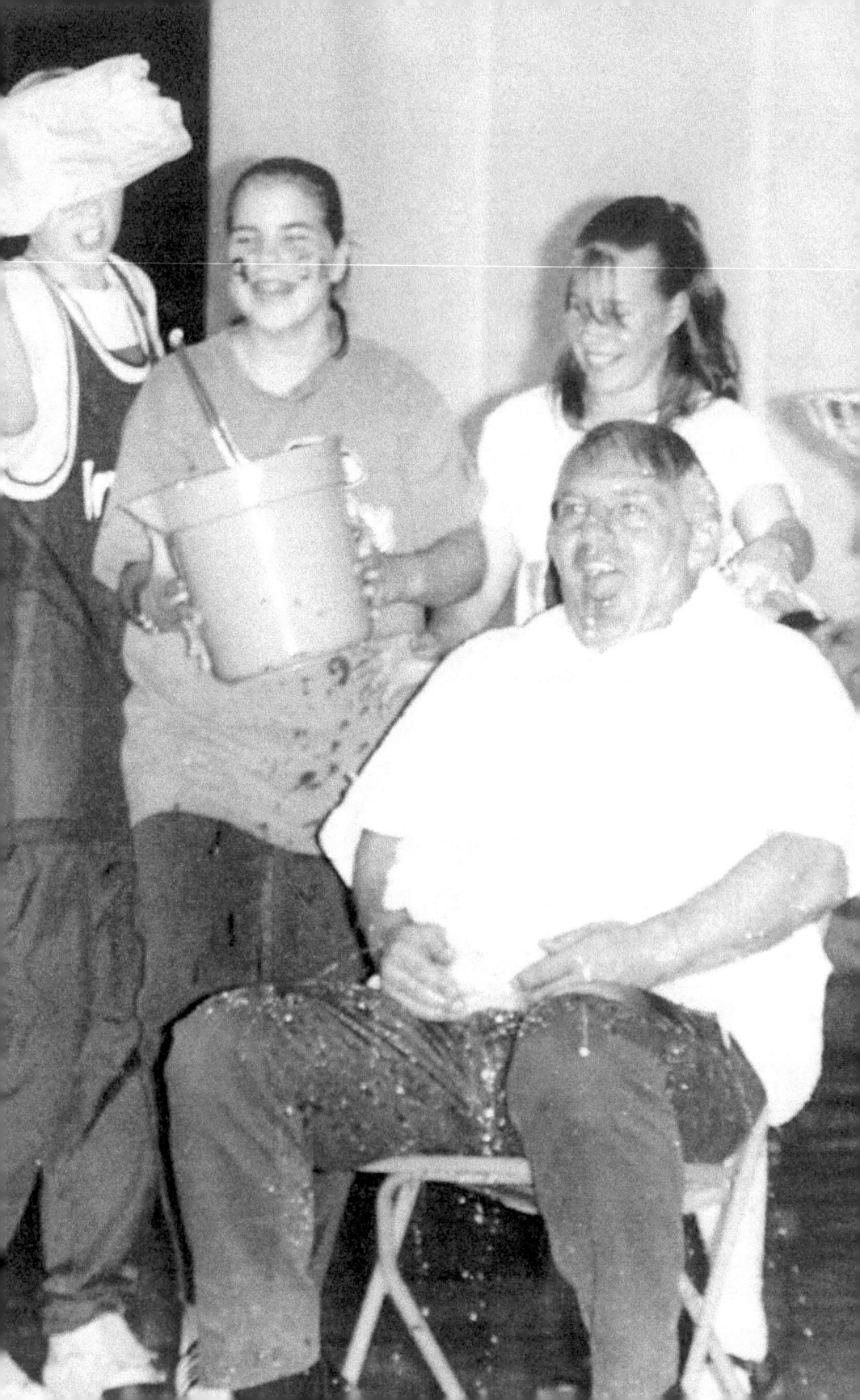

8

HIGHLAND PARK JUNIOR HIGH

My Little Family
(1975–1989)

THE NEXT FEW YEARS JUST SEEMED TO FLY BY, with great moments and some real learning experiences. After my first year of teaching, Debbie and I decided to get married. Before the wedding—on August 1, 1975—Debbie and I decided to sell our Volkswagens and buy a 914 Porsche for our honeymoon. We took delivery about a week before the wedding, and after the ceremony headed down along the coast to California. It was fun, but I was always afraid someone was going to steal the 914, and my anxiety was running high.

A year later, we were expecting our first child, so we said good-bye to the Porsche and bought a new Toyota Celica. We needed room for Kristyn, our little girl. We used some of the money from the sale of the Porsche to buy our first house in Cedar Hills. We didn't want to bring our child up in an apartment. This house was a three-bedroom ranch, with the garage converted into a family room. It was in nice shape, and a good starter home.

When Kristyn Marie came along, she was a wonderful addition to our lives. She was not only beautiful, but a very caring, thoughtful girl. She was solid in her actions toward others.

It was amazing to watch how quickly Debbie adapted to life as a full-time mom, and how comfortable she was raising our child. On the other hand, I always felt anxiety, and worried about Kristyn getting hurt. To say the least, I was a very protective father.

A few years later, Heather Nicole came along, with her wonderful sense of humor. I will never forget Heather's little joke on me. I would be in the bathroom, sitting on the toilet. Heather would knock on the door and say, "Whatcha doin' in there, Dad?" Then she would run down the hall, laughing all the way. A few minutes later there would be another knock, and she would do it all over again, laughing so everyone knew what she was up to. She thought this was a great way to tease her dad.

They were both beautiful girls, and I love them both to this day, and always will. I will always admire Debbie for the great job she did as their mother. She was a very smart lady, and both my girls inherited her intelligence and wonderful smile.

Highland Park Junior High
(1974–1987)

MY FIRST YEAR AS A HEAD JUNIOR HIGH SCHOOL football coach proved to be a real learning experience. To be quite honest, I had no clue what I was doing. I was learning as I went. As time went on, certain basic principles of football jumped out me. I slowly figured it out. It dawned on me to just keep it simple, and do a few plays and defenses well, rather than doing a lot of them poorly. I have realized over the years that there is no short-cut to performing well. Just like being ready for that test in school, my teams needed to be ready to play on game day.

I also enjoyed the kids. They could see how much I loved football. They knew I wanted them to be successful and enjoy victory, but also to learn from defeat. There was no question in my mind that football could teach these young athletes to be strong and honest in life. Yes, I worried about them getting hurt—but the attributes and skills that they gained on that football field were worth the risk.

I was also the head baseball coach. I had little trouble putting players in the right frame of mind to play well. Even though I was a better football player, baseball coaching had already become one of my strengths. During college in the summer months I had coached eight little-league teams; all had won the league championships at their level. For several years, coaching baseball at Highland Park was great fun, and a wonderful continuation of baseball and league championships.

Over the years I worked hard at Highland Park, creating a lot of spirit in the school. I always thought school should not only be a learning experience in the classroom, but also in the many activities a school offers. I was good at putting on large assemblies that would charge up the kids and the teachers. This created a fun and positive school environment. I guess my reward was that the kids showed how much they appreciated my hard work. Students voted me best teacher one year, funniest teacher the next, and best lecturer the year after that. I also was asked to do some TV appearances by Channel 8 and Channel 6 News in Portland, on my health classes, which concerned our young students' sexuality and values.

Even though I was doing well teaching and coaching, had two wonderful children and a caring wife, my marriage was suffering. My trust issues were always there. I didn't know why. I would wander the house at night, looking out the windows to see if everything was safe. Whenever we traveled, my anxiety prevented my enjoyment of the trip. I just wanted to be back home and safe. My wife would be in tears, because she couldn't understand why I was acting the way I was—always mistrusting her and not having fun. To say the least, it was not good. The only thing I knew was that as long as I was in a routine, I would do better. The accident on the *USS Mars* still haunted me, growing and feeding my mistrust and fear. Trauma is not only frightening at the time, but afterward: it can be the start of a continuing battleground of wars you fight inside yourself. I am still fighting these wars today.

Classroom Room B-14

In the early years of my teaching career, I spent a lot of time in classroom B-14 at Highland Park Junior High, in Beaverton, Oregon. When I arrived at Highland, I was hired as a PE teacher, but soon our principal decided that I would be moved to the ninth-grade health program. I was not very happy about the move, and very uncomfortable with students seeing a side of me that wasn't very polished in the classroom. There was no question that my spelling, grammar, and reading abilities needed improvement. I was going to be in front of a total of 180 students for six periods every day. The thought of making a fool of myself was not very comforting.

For whatever reason, I believed I was called to teach; not because of my knowledge from books, but for having an ability or gift to communicate with young people in a sincere way. I had acquired the ability to move kids in a good direction, whether in a large assembly or individually. My approach was simple and conservative and easy to follow. I wanted my classes to be fun, exciting, and informative. I felt that my health classes needed to be a place where students could ask questions about their well-being, and where all topics would be open for discussion. Most important, I wanted them to respect each other and follow classroom rules for the benefit of all. Because of my background, I brought many life stories that I could share with the students—some related to health, and some just to break the humdrum of school. I think the students enjoyed the stories, and I hope when you read this book you will too. My students had fun learning, and had a laugh or two along the way.

As a child, I was left to grow up pretty much on my own. Because of that, I had a certain sensitivity to students who might be hurting inside or feeling bad about themselves. When I looked over my classroom, these students seemed to jump out at me. I guess I knew their pain; I had felt their pain too. It was important to me to spend time with these students and get to know them. All my students understood that I was not there to be their friend, but to help them. They knew that I really cared about their future. I tried to help in any way I could. This will help readers understand who I was, and that good teachers come from many different places. Going to college and getting great grades is just *part* of what teachers need. I believe that great teachers are called to the profession to help kids achieve their highest potential.

My teaching career probably started when I was about eight years old. I would organize the kids in the neighborhood and we would all go up to the grade school and play baseball. Then there were hours of basketball games in front of our house. My teams would win, and because of that, kids wanted to be with me, so they could be part of the winning. I guess another part of winning was my love of working hard, and having the belief that you could win if you worked hard. I recall coming in the house after playing basketball outside. I was dripping wet in sweat. My mother couldn't believe it. I would go to the refrigerator, down a half gallon of milk, and then immediately return for another round of action outside. I would play for hours, and then be dead tired until the next day, when it started all over again.

As I got older, I gained a certain amount of respect from my peers for being a good high school football player and all-around athlete. After graduation from high school and failing my first attempt at junior college, I found myself once again put in a position of leadership and teaching. I had enlisted in the US Navy, and shortly after arriving at boot camp, I was picked to command the other forty recruits in my company for the next eight weeks. Once again, I was put in a teaching position, and a competitive situation. I was able to lead those forty men to become the honor company, and to receive numerous awards.

After my release from military service, I attended Linfield College in McMinnville, Oregon, where I decided to become a teacher. While at Linfield, I worked on my degree, and played college baseball and football. I was a catcher on the JV baseball team, and while catching, directed the rest of the team during the games. During the summers, while attending Linfield, I worked for Tualatin Hills Parks and Recreation in Beaverton, Oregon; there, I coached three little-league teams at once. So in actuality, I was already teaching. My little-league teams were good, and as I pushed the kids to work hard, they did. It appeared that I had developed a teaching philosophy before I ever entered a classroom. In baseball, we practiced situations over and over, and as I applied pressure or accountability to the situations, it helped players adapt and perform at a higher level. Over time and after many hours of repetition, players became comfortable under pressure, and played well.

The bottom line was that applying a high level of pressure and accountability in practice was one of the keys to my team's success. During games, if a mistake was made, it was played down, and nothing but a positive approach was used. The players were prepared for games, and a positive tone was set. They played hard, and whether we won or lost, I thanked them for their efforts.

He Just Wanted to Play

My first story is about one of my first little-league baseball teams, and a kid by the name of Mike Duffy. Mike played second base on one of my summer teams while I was attending Linfield College. He was quite an inspiration to me, and to the rest of the players as well. When I first saw Mike take the field, he had kind of a different walk—and even more so when he broke into a run toward his position at second base. When I first hit a grounder to him, it went right through his legs, and then he turned and ran after the ball, picking it up in time to make the throw to first base. He then hustled back to his position and was immediately ready for the next play. He was enthusiastic, and you could tell he was a worker and a hustler.

I found out later that Mike was hindered by two plastic hip sockets, which made it hard for him to run and bend over to catch a grounder. It didn't matter to Mike—he just wanted to play. I don't think he ever thought of giving up or not trying his best. I can't count the number of times this kid dove for the ball. Somehow he always came up with it and made the play—to the cheers and delight of the parents and his fellow players. The other teams would just shake their heads in disbelief at the effort Mike had shown. Mike went on to become an assistant football coach at Portland State University.

That particular group of boys was made up of the players left over from not making the first two teams, and given to me for a third team because they weren't very good. I could tell very quickly that we were in big trouble—but the good news was these kids *wanted* to play baseball. One day early in the season, I realized we needed a good pitcher. To my delight, I found him riding his bike up the street. Neil was big and strong and wore a huge smile that went from cheek to cheek. As he stopped and parked his bike and then sat in the bleachers to watch practice, I called him over. I asked if he would like to play and maybe try out for the team. He responded with a yes, so I asked him to grab a bat to see if he could hit the ball. Neil picked up the bat, and when I pitched the ball he took a swing. As I watched the ball fly over the fence, leaving the park, I got a big smile on my face—and so did the rest of the players.

I asked Neil if he could pitch, and once again he responded with a yes. I gave him the baseball and let him throw a few pitches. As he struck out the batters, I knew my prayers had been answered. I called the team over and asked how they would feel about Neil coming on board with us. They all agreed, and the stage was set for a great summer in baseball. We practiced hard, catching fly balls and grounders. Every time a player missed the ball or made a bad throw, he was given five pushups. We practiced hitting the ball hard, laying down perfect bunts over and over until we started to do it right. I taught the kids aggressive base-running, how to slide, the art of the double steal, and even delayed steals. I pushed them to make perfect throws from the outfield and perfect throws in the infield. Most important, we practiced situations so players knew what to do and when to do it.

It took some time, but after a while the team looked completely different from when we had started with our first practice. When it came time for our first game, we won—it wasn't even close. I don't think the parents could believe these were their kids. Mike Duffy made outstanding plays at second; Neil struck out batters and hit home runs. Our outfielders caught fly balls, it was a great start, and from that game on they just got better and better. This group of players had big hearts and went on to an undefeated season. Even though they lost their last game in the playoffs to a team that was a division higher, they proved to everyone that they were true winners, and that they loved the game of baseball.

Here Come the Police

ONE DAY, AS MY BASEBALL TEAM GATHERED FOR practice, I told them that we were going down to Civic Stadium in Portland—where the Portland Beavers played—for our practice. The players looked at each other and started cheering. I had acquired a station wagon to drive down to the stadium. On the way, Rick, our shortstop, who was sitting in the "way-back" of the car, ducked down and started to make the sound of a police siren coming our way.

When I heard the siren, I immediately pulled the car over to the side of the road and waited for the police car to pass. As I waited, there was no police car in sight. I then pulled back onto the road to continue our drive toward the stadium. A short time later, I heard another police siren. Once again I pulled over to side of the road and waited for the police car to pass—and once again there was nothing.

I looked at the kids. They all seemed to have a funny smile on their faces, which seemed odd to me. Once again, I pulled out, and after a few moments I heard another siren from the rear of the station wagon. This time, the kids couldn't keep a straight face—they all started laughing. Rick, the shortstop, was in the back, imitating the police siren perfectly. Then we all started laughing. For the rest of the season, every once in a while, I would hear Rick sounding off with the siren, and everyone would start to laugh.

I continued to develop my teaching abilities with many other little-league teams during the summers while attending Linfield. They all went undefeated, improving with hard work. When summer was over. I reported back to Linfield to play college football. As I have stated earlier, my main goal was to work harder than anyone else on the field. At the start of the football season, I always started out strong. I was in tremendous shape when football practices started. Then I would play so hard my body would start to break down, and I would get hurt or sick and miss games. Even though at the first part of every season, I played at a high level and attained some college records, I honestly believe that trying so hard kept me from All-American honors. I can remember players in practice getting upset at me because I would try so hard. I'm not sure they understood that it was just my nature, and that I loved competing.

Later, I realized I had missed too many games from illness and broken bones to be considered for All-American. My point is just this: you can try *too* hard. I think if teachers and coaches can teach young people how to regulate their efforts for the long haul, students and players will perform longer and more consistently. When students feel comfortable and rested they are in a great mindset—they will retain more knowledge and perform at a higher level. I missed my chance to reach my potential on the field. I was not aware of the importance of pacing myself. I lost my chance to be recognized as the athlete I had worked so hard to become, simply because I needed to slow down.

Mr. Geigle's Assemblies

DURING MY DAYS AT LINFIELD COLLEGE, I HAD A friend by the name of Mark Holly. Mark was also an offensive lineman on the football team. He was a great guy, and was always trying to make fun of a moment or situation. He was good at helping me regain my sense of humor, which had been locked away since my accident on the ship.

Every year, the students at Linfield would put on a show known as the "Linfield Follies." It was a talent show, where anyone could get on stage and demonstrate their talent. Mark and I were picked to be the masters of ceremony. I was the straight guy and Mark would come up with some smart and funny comment to anything I would say. We both enjoyed the chance to ham it up. Mark would say, "I was a pilot on a cattle ranch." Then I might say, "Really?" Mark would come back and say, "Yeah—I'd pile it here, then I'd pile it over there"—pointing to the different locations he was piling cow dung. You would hear groans from the audience. Then we would introduce the next act.

After college and after becoming a teacher at Highland Park Junior High School in Beaverton. I decided to promote school spirit by putting together Spirit Assemblies, which improved our school atmosphere. I involved students, teachers, and even the principal to perform in front of the rest of the student body. Every holiday assembly, I would play Santa Claus. I would come rolling out of a fireplace, constructed by the students, with a mighty, "Ho, ho, ho," and parade around the gym with my elves—handing out candy, waving, and saying "Merry Christmas." The students loved this.

We would also take pictures of the students around school, a few weeks before the assembly. I would then have slides made and project them on the gym wall during the assembly, as Christmas music played in the background. When the kids saw themselves with their friends, they cheered. One year, playing Santa, I was sitting on a tall chair, giving out awards. When I started to give an award to the math teacher, he came running down from the bleachers and jumped in my lap—and we both went over backwards in the chair, which ignited the students in laughter. It was all in fun!

Those assemblies were highly successful and brought praise from students and faculty. The students honored my efforts by voting me Spirit King in 1983, Best Lecture 1984, and Funniest Teacher in 1985. For the next twenty years I used the Spirit Assemblies to help create a positive school atmosphere, wherever I taught.

These assemblies were put on with a lot of help from kids who were hurting or shy, and sometimes just lonely. I always felt that no child should feel left out. My assemblies helped them feel special. They loved helping me, and it changed them. Junior high can be a difficult time, and I could see many of these kids literally coming out of their protective shells to be part of something. They could see that a teacher, Mr. Geigle, really cared about them. Because I had a wild and interesting childhood, I could bring part of that experience, energy, and creativity to students in a sincere, fun, and healthy way. My love for children overshadowed any weakness I had as a teacher. They had respect for me simply because I had respect for them, which was genuine and heartfelt.

A Boy Named Joe

THIS NEXT STORY IS ABOUT A BOY NAMED JOE. JOE came from a family with four very large sons. Joe's dad was six foot seven and a mountain of a man. Joe's brothers—Pete, Stan, and Willie—were just like their father: big, strong, and fast. All three boys played college and then pro football. When Joe became one of my students in the ninth grade at Highland Park, he wanted to be like his big brothers and play football. Joe had a learning disability, but made up for it with his sense of humor and enthusiasm.

During the school year, Joe helped me with a fundraiser by putting on a haunted house. We set up a fake operation in the boys' PE dressing room in the teachers' office. Joe played a doctor operating on someone who was lying on an operating table under a blue light. He used hamburger as bloody guts, and had also made an hour-long recording of a heartbeat, using his own voice for the sound effects. He played the heartbeat as people walked by and looked through the window, watching him operate. Then he would slowly turn and look at them, while walking towards the door, to open it as if to grab one of them—like a mad scientist. It looked like the real thing. The haunted house made over two thousand dollars that night, and Joe was the big hit.

Joe's learning handicap prompted a tough discussion on whether it was safe for him to play football. As the head football coach, I could see the sadness that Joe was feeling by being told he couldn't play. At that time, we had two ninth-grade football teams. One team was made up of bigger players and the other team was smaller players. We did this to make the games safer and more competitive. After getting to know Joe, I knew that even though he was a tall kid, his disability meant that he would fit right in with the smaller team. Getting permission for him to play wasn't easy. Explaining to the staff why Joe should have a chance to be like his brothers wasn't easy.

When I finally convinced the staff to allow Joe to try out for the team, and told him so, his eyes lit up and he walked around the school, proud that he was going to be a football player. When practice started, I kept a close eye on him, making sure he was practicing with players close to his ability. The first time Joe was knocked down in a blocking drill, he started to cry. He just lay there on the ground, weeping. I told all the players to move ten yards down the field, and continued the drill. I told Joe that when he was done crying, the team would be downfield, and to get up and get back in line. I also told him, "Welcome to football."

After a while, I watched as he got to his feet and got back in line for the drill. When it was his turn again, he got knocked down.

Again he started to cry—so again I moved the team. This time I didn't say a word. I was letting Joe decide whether he was going to play football or not. Joe got up, got back in line, and was ready, once again, for his turn. This time, I told Joe that he needed to knock the whoop-tee-do out of the other player. You could see the determination in his eyes. When the ball was hiked and the two players came together, Joe drove his opponent ten yards down the field. The other players went crazy, cheering Joe on, then surrounding him, patting him on the back and telling him what a great job he had done. Joe was smiling from ear to ear. He never cried again.

Joe went on to be the starting right-tackle for the lightweight team, and had a wonderful season. He was voted Most Inspirational Player by his teammates. He never played football again after that year, but we all knew it had changed him forever. Joe's family thanked me for all I had done. In the spring, Joe became my baseball equipment manager and did a tremendous job—always wearing a big smile. I loved that guy!

Community Service

AS TIME WENT ON IN ROOM B-14, AT HIGHLAND PARK, I decided to use my classroom to teach not only health, but also programs that would help students practice good citizenship. At the end of every period, I would assign a job for the students to perform to help clean up the classroom. I also sent students into the hallways to pick up trash and make sure the school was clean. The custodians loved this and it set an example for the rest of the school. Students would receive a community service grade at the end of the nine weeks. If they had shown respect to each other and done well on the classroom clean-up, it could really help their grade. I gave extra credit for community service—like performing in assemblies, attending school activities, helping with canned-food drives, and reporting to the class regarding current health events from newspapers and magazines.

There were many ways to pass the class and at the same time help your school. I would thank them for their hard work and effort. Sometimes on Fridays we would have donut day. Students loved this! I would take orders, then pick up the donuts before school and hand them out during free time.

The Rowdy Raiders

THE ROWDY RAIDERS WERE A GROUP OF KIDS WHO wanted to be a part of some type of activity in the school. They weren't interested in playing a sport, but enjoyed being loud at the games. If you were a Rowdy Raider, on game day, your job was to dress up in a suit and tie and carry a suitcase. You were then to show up at school with a group of twenty to thirty students. People would think you were headed away for a long weekend. At a certain time, the Rowdy Raiders would meet in front of the school. Then they would walk down the hall and enter the gym, singing the Highland Park fight song. It went like this: "Fight, fight, fight for old Highland Park. Win a vic-to-ry. We're going to fight, fight, fight for the best in the west. So on, on, on to the end. Win a vic-to-ry. We're going to fight, fight, fight for old Highland Park and vic-to-ry."

Their sole purpose was to be loud and rowdy, cheering on their home team. They also supported the cheerleaders, and even memorized a few of their own special cheers. During a time-out or pause in the action, they would all stand up together and sing the Highland Park fight song, once again. If one of the players on Highland's team did something outstanding, they all stood up and cheered them on. I made a point to make sure they showed good sportsmanship, but they were certainly rowdy. Everyone loved it except the other team. The Rowdy Raider students became known throughout the school during a basketball season. It was fun, and a great example of school spirit. Once again, this activity put students onstage who normally wouldn't have taken the chance.

Coachbear 30

DURING MY DAYS AT HIGHLAND PARK AS THE HEAD football coach, I was given the nickname "Coachbear." If you happened to wander out to the football field when the team was practicing, you couldn't help but hear or see me yelling. I guess I sounded and looked like a big old bear in the woods. My hair would be flying in the wind, as I pushed the kids toward perfection. I would try to set a tone for working hard in practice. If a player did something great, everybody for half a mile could hear my praise. If the team was dogging it, you could hear my unhappiness about that, also.

Even today, when I watch my grandson play, he has no problem hearing Grampa cheering him on. It was the same in baseball—I wanted their best, every day and every practice. "The Bear" wouldn't settle for less.

When computers became popular, I needed an email address. So I have always used "Coachbear30" as the beginning of my email address. Thirty is my old high school football number, so I just tacked it onto "Coachbear." The kids in school, as the years went on, mostly called me "Coach Geigle," out of respect—but they all knew the Bear, at times. Even today, the Bear will fire up, if he needs to.

Safeco Summertime Claims Adjuster

BECAUSE TEACHERS WERE NOT PAID WELL BACK IN the 70s and 80s, I took on extra jobs to supplement my income. Sometimes I would do paper routes with my car in the early mornings before going to teach and coach. Often, I would be up at 4 a.m., deliver 500 newspapers, take a short thirty-minute nap, and then go teach a full day of school—coaching football or baseball after that. In the summers I would paint houses and do a little landscaping. Finally, I also worked as a summer "storm trooper" (not to be confused with stormtroopers from *Star Wars*) for Safeco Insurance Company. I don't know where the energy came from, but being busy kept my mind off my fear and anxiety.

Working for Safeco was a great experience. Even today, I am thankful for those summers that I traveled for them. I would fly to different parts of the country, where a major hailstorm or hurricane had occurred, estimate damages to insured property, and write a check for those damages. Sometimes I would be gone two or three weeks, and then return home and handle local claims until the next storm occurred. The travel was very hard for me—it turned out to be my undoing with this job, even though I loved the work.

One of my greatest moments with this summer work happened while I was inspecting an insurance claim from a major hailstorm in Colorado Springs, Colorado. When I arrived at the client's house, he greeted me and indicated that after looking up at his roof he really didn't see any major damage. I asked him if he had been up on the roof, and he said, "No". I said, "Let me go up so we can be sure there is no hail damage." He agreed.

A few minutes later I saw the small holes all over his roof. After my inspection I got down and told him about the holes. I told him we owed him for the damages, and we would replace the entire roof. He couldn't believe how well he was being treated, and told me how grateful he was. I wrote him a large check for the damages, and said, "Have a great day." Then I went on my way.

A few hours later, I received a call from my boss, who thanked me for doing such a fine job. The guy with the roof had called. He was so happy that he had cancelled his large company's insurance plan with another carrier, rewriting his entire company insurance policy with Safeco. This meant huge gains of thousands of dollars of premium for Safeco. I always felt that it was important to be honest and help folks who were suffering a loss; getting them back on their feet. It seemed like the right thing to do. I was just doing my job. Safeco was a very conservative insurance company. I mean, they wore white shirts and ties every day, and watched every penny. But the bottom line was that I put the customer first, and so did Safeco.

CHAPTER NINE
A NEW CAREER

The Jerk
(1987)

AFTER MANY YEARS OF THESE SECOND AND
third jobs I was getting pretty worn out. I started looking in the paper for a job that would pay more money so I wouldn't have to work
so hard. As I looked, I came across American Fidelity Insurance
Company. I called, went in for an interview, and liked what I heard.
I went home, told my wife, and decided I could always come back
to being a teacher and coach.

The next thing I knew, I was flying to Oklahoma for three weeks of
training before receiving my new company car and expense account.
My new job was to sell large group medical and life insurance in the
state of Oregon. Before starting on my own, I traveled around the
state for two weeks with my new boss. Soon, I would realize that he

was one of the biggest jerks I ever met in my working career. One day he turned to me and said, "Are you going to sell something or not?" I looked at him and told him he was a jerk. I said, "Get back on the plane and go back to Oklahoma. I also told him that if I didn't perform well, he could fire me. I dropped him off at the airport and started my new adventure, already having concerns about the company I worked for.

There were so many important things to know about sales that I was unaware of. But one thing I did know was not to give up. When I took the State Insurance License test, I failed to pass it twice. On the third try, I knew the questions so well that I passed.

After a good six weeks in this new job, I knew I had made a mistake. Every morning when I got up, I had to figure out where to go and sell insurance. I hated it, and it wasn't easy—especially when you didn't have good support. At the end of the first year, I flew back to Oklahoma City and attended the end-of-the-year sales meeting. When I walked in, I couldn't believe what I saw. Up in front of this large room was a giant, blown-up picture of me. I immediately wondered why. Soon, the meeting started, and it was announced that I was the leading salesman in the company that year. I thought to myself, *What a joke—I haven't sold squat.* Then I remembered that I had been selling small, twenty-five-dollar-a-month, term life insurance to everyone I met. I again thought to myself, *If that's all I've done, what the heck are all these salesman doing? Playing golf all day?* Right at that moment, I smiled and told myself, *I'm done with this job. This company is a joke!* I flew back home, broke the news to my wife, and started looking.

Two weeks later, I was asked to go to lunch with the Jerk. He knew I was unhappy. We met at the airport and sat down for lunch. He didn't waste any time, and told me I was fired. He said that I would receive two weeks' pay and the use of the company car for that time. I was upset, but also relieved. I got up and walked away—never looking back.

Back To Safeco

Since I had worked for Safeco Insurance Company I stopped by their office on the way home from meeting with the Jerk. I spoke with the people who had known me from the past summers, and before I left, they had hired me. I had my new job. My wife was relieved, and so was I. I was happy to be working at Safeco.

After two weeks of training, I got another new company car and a new expense account. I was now a full-time Physical Damage My job was, once again, to estimate damage to automobiles and property. It was great, and I knew where to go every day. I loved consistency! For the next three years, I worked for Safeco. It was a much better experience in a true professional atmosphere. It was hard work for me, but it kept me busy and my family fed.

My second greatest experience with Safeco occurred when I went to see an auto claim in Portland. Our insured had just purchased a brand-new Mercedes. A few days later, while parked at a Blazer game, someone side-swiped his car. The insured was very upset, and wanted Safeco to buy him a new Mercedes. After writing an estimate for damages, and talking to the upset owner, I went back to the office to talk with my boss about what Safeco should pay for the damages. He said the only thing we were responsible for was repairing the damage so that the car was as good as before the accident. Later, I called the owner and explained the situation. He was still very upset, since the car wasn't even a week old. I thought for a moment, and then I said, "Go down to the Mercedes dealer where you purchased the car, and ask them what the car would be worth once the damages were repaired." I knew the Mercedes dealer would say the car was worth nothing, because it had been damaged. They would not touch it because of it's diminished value. I also told the owner to ask for a letter stating their position on the car.

He thanked me, and a few days later submitted a letter indicating his car had no value and that they would not touch it. When my boss saw the letter, he said, "Pay the owner to buy a new Mercedes, and we will sell the damaged car for salvage and get what we can to recover our loss." So the owner of the Mercedes got a brand-new car, and thanked me over and over again. Once again, I had put the insured first, and found a way to justify how I had settled the claim.

A few weeks later there was a package on my doorstep—no name, no address. When I opened it up, it had been filled to the top with sunglasses of all colors and styles. I never found out where that package had come from, but I had a good idea. My family didn't buy sunglasses for years after that.

During my time at Safeco, my wife Debbie and I decided to throw in the towel on our relationship and get a divorce. It was a real hard time for me. I suffered many panic attacks and continued anxiety from it. I was real good at hiding my trauma symptoms, because I wanted everything to be normal. It got to a point where I would try to go for a walk, and ended up with an upset stomach, feeling nauseous and scared. I would go back inside, try to eat something to settle my stomach, and feel my heart racing. It was always a feeling of panic and fear!

One day while sitting at my desk at Safeco, the phone rang. It was my old principal from Highland Park. After talking awhile, he asked how I was doing, and whether I would be interested in coming back to teaching and coaching. I thought for a half a second, and then said, "Yes!" He told me to come in for an interview the next day, which I did. And what do you know? Two weeks later, I was a teacher again, at Five Oaks Middle School. I said goodbye to Safeco—very thankful for what they had done for me.

10

A NEW BEGINNING

The Long Road Back to Teaching and Coaching

MY NEW TEACHING ASSIGNMENT WAS AT FIVE Oaks Junior High in my old school district: Beaverton, Oregon. But as soon as I arrived and met the PE teachers, I realized that I was not welcome. Sam, my old principal, had hired me while the two women PE teachers were away on summer vacation. But they both had someone else all picked out for the job. From day one, these two ladies had it in for me. So it didn't matter how well I did—they wanted me gone. When I think about it now, many years later, I believe they were liberal in their way of thinking, while I was "old school," or conservative. Our teaching styles clashed.

As the year went on, I was asked to help coach football. I had, at one time years before, coached against Five Oaks, at Highland Park. After a few days, I could see areas concerning line-blocking schemes that were weak. We changed them, and it helped a lot. I could see the coaches' and students' respect for me growing, because I knew football and they could see that. Because they hadn't been very strong in football, they were excited that we were having a winning season, and felt good about my helping.

After football was over, a few weeks later I was asked to coach the boys' JV basketball team, which had a losing tradition that spanned ten years. My only experience coaching basketball at the time was two girls' teams that I had coached years before. Both teams had gone undefeated, winning their leagues. I decided to go ahead and coach the boys, even though I didn't know too much about what I was doing.

During the first practice I took a look at the talent I was given and could see some bright spots. We worked hard. I've got to say, it was fun for me as well as the players. It wasn't long before my players started to believe in my aggressive, conservative style of play. We got better and better, and soon word got out, and people were coming to watch the JV team winning games. We ended up losing only one game that year, to a team that had beat us the first time we played. But toward the end of the season we beat them, and won the league title. I was really proud of what the kids had done, and so were their parents. The team had earned some respect—not only from their opponents, but from other students and staff members at Five Oaks.

Of course, the two women PE teachers still didn't approve of me, and told the principal that I was too aggressive, and should be coaching high school. I'll never forget those two teachers. Maybe they were just afraid because the basketball team had won for the first time in ten years, and this new teacher was becoming too popular. Well, they got their way. At the end of the year, the principal called me in and said I wouldn't be returning. He made it clear that he didn't want to let me go, but was trying to keep the peace with these two other teachers. Since I was a first-year temporary teacher, I couldn't argue. And to be quite honest, I was realizing that I was different now, and wanted to coach and teach older kids.

I spent the next two weeks looking for something I could do before the money ran out. I ran across an opening at Tualatin Parks and Recreation in Beaverton, Oregon—in Cedar Hills, where I grew up. They needed a part-time evening supervisor for the Cedar Hills Recreation Center. I had worked as a part-time gym supervisor a few years before, and had done a pretty good job. I applied and got the job. I was in good spirits, as they had always treated me well. The job didn't pay much, but I had reduced my debt, and did the best I could with what I earned.

When I started working there, I realized very quickly that I was surrounded by really great people. Linda, who was my boss, quickly earned my respect. To this day, she is still one of the greatest supervisors I ever had. She was positive, and seemed to bring the best out of her employees on a daily basis. Anyway, from 3 p.m. until 10 p.m. every day, I was in charge of the Cedar Hills Rec Center.

I always felt that people didn't come to the recreation center for trouble. They were there to relax and even laugh if they could. I became good at bringing smiles to their faces, and helping them in any way I could. It was a good fit, and it worked out well. So for the next few months, I had some real fun at work.

But because that job was part-time, and only paid ten dollars an hour, I had to keep looking for full-time work. When the new school year started, I applied to be a substitute teacher in the mornings for the Beaverton School District. I waited for my first call to be a substitute—I wanted to get back into education.

On to Grant High School
(1990)

A T THE END OF THE SUMMER AND THE START OF THE new school year I started substituting again—landing at Sunset High School, where I had graduated from. I was there to fill in for Coach Ken Harris, who was also the athletic director. He taught two PE classes in the morning, and worked on athletics the rest of the day.

After I filled in for him for a few days, he thanked me for doing a great job. He also said that the students enjoyed my teaching, and were making positive comments about my classroom atmosphere. This all sounded good to me. It was great teaching older kids.

After coming back in for Coach Harris again a few days later, the office called me down. The principal complimented me on my classroom management and classroom atmosphere. Along with the compliment, he also asked me to call Grant High School in the Portland Public School District. He said they had heard about me, and would like to interview me for a position. After the meeting, I thanked him, and called Grant. They asked me to come in the next day. After the interview, I waited for a call. Later that week, the phone rang, and I was offered a half-time teaching position as a personal finance teacher. I would only be teaching two classes of personal finance—which sounds easy, except that I had no clue or experience in the subject area. Even though it would be hard, I was thankful for the opportunity.

I remember how different Grant High School was, compared to other schools I had taught at. It was an enormous, brick building that had three levels. At one time, it had been the "showcase" of ed-ucation in Oregon. Some of the richest people in the state had sent their children there. As I walked the halls, I could sense the years of history, and the thousands of students who had attended this school, and become successful and famous.

One of the teachers I met and grew to know very well was Bill Siler. He worked in the math department, and was a few years from the end of his career. Bill had been a head high school football coach, and highly successful in the Southern Oregon League. Bill had also written a book, *The Bulldog Defense*. He was about five foot six, and had played quarterback for the University of Washington, taking them to the Rose Bowl in the early 60s. Even though he was short, you knew without question he was tough as nails. He was a truly seasoned teacher, to say the least. I miss him to this day. He was real, and did not mince words. We talked every day at lunch about coaching and my dream of becoming a head football coach at the high-school level. He didn't know about (and I never brought up) my trauma issues, and how they were keeping me from fulfilling my coaching dream. We parted as good friends when I moved. I will always remember him as one of the best educators and people I met in my career.

The Wild Bunch

AT THE END OF THE FIRST SEMESTER AT GRANT, I WAS called down to the office, and the principal offered me a full-time position with the Bridge Program.

The Bridge Program was a large group of students who were at risk of not graduating. My job was to make sure they graduated—helping them with their schoolwork, study habits, behavior, and self-confidence. Because going through school had been tough for me, I felt this might be a good fit for both the students and me. After being told what the class was about, I accepted the position. Since it was full-time, I had to resign my position at the recreation center, so I gave my two weeks' notice. I was sad to leave such great people, but it was time to move on.

The Bridge Program was made up of mostly black students who were living very tough lives and really hadn't had the necessary support at home. I didn't know it at the time, but I would be their teacher for the next four years. It would be my toughest four years in education. It didn't take me long to realize that I was out of my comfort zone. Even though I worked hard to create a positive environment, at the end of the day the students would go home to poverty. Sometimes I would see a student with bandages on his body and would ask what had happened. The student would reply that he had been shot or stabbed or beaten up. It was hard for me to understand this type of continuing negativity. I really didn't like the job after a while, but I was committed to giving it my best, and I truly tried to do just that.

Lee Lander's Big Night Out

ONE OF MY FAVORITE STORIES IS ABOUT A YOUNG student in the Bridge Program. His name was Lee, and he was not doing well in school, and had somewhat of a behavioral problem. I knew if his effort in school didn't improve he wasn't going to graduate.

One day in class I pulled Lee aside and started talking to him. I could see he wasn't paying attention to me. What I was saying was going in one ear and out the other. All of a sudden I had an idea. I said, "Lee, I know you really like my car." His eyes got bigger as I went on. "Lee, if you get your grades up to a three point by the end of this semester, I'll let you drive my car to the prom. I will come over, talk with your parents, get it approved with them and the insurance company, and it will be yours for the prom."

At the time, my car was a 1990 BMW convertible, gun-metal blue. It was perfect, to say the least, and Lee knew it. He couldn't believe what he was hearing. He couldn't believe a teacher would do something that crazy. He got all excited, and a big smile lit up his face. Well, guess what happened? Lee not only got a 3.0—the following quarter, he ran for student body office. I can still remember getting a call on the Thursday night before the prom—the prom was going to be on Saturday night—and the sound of Lee's voice. "Mr. Geigle," he said, "do you think I could have the car Friday night, to wash it and get it ready?" There was a long moment of silence. Then I told him, "Sure, why not?" I never saw a kid so excited, especially when I handed him the keys, in front of his parents, standing in his living room. Lee went on his big night out, went to the dance, and returned the car to me on Sunday without a scratch. (Thank God!) That one event proved to be the turning point in his high school career. He went on to graduate the next year. My relationship with him had been completely changed by that one act of kindness.

Many years later I ran into Lee at a 7-Eleven. He was driving a delivery truck and doing well. We laughed about him using my car for the prom and kidded around a little. I realized very quickly that he was still a great kid, and that I would not forget him. Because the Bridge students were at risk of dropping out of school. I tried to come up with different ideas to motivate and reward them for getting their work turned in. Every week they would carry a progress report to all their classes. If the report came back acceptable, then on Friday morning, I would walk them over to McDonalds' and buy breakfast. They loved it, and worked hard during the week just to take the walk to Mickey D's with me. I found that these types of positive rewards helped them stay focused. It also let them know that I was trying, and that I cared.

Scappoose Middle School
(1995–1997)

AFTER FOUR YEARS, I LEFT GRANT AND WAS READY for a new adventure and maybe some coaching. But during the summer months of 1995, I was still a teacher at Grant High School and looking for a new position. One day I received a call from my brother Steve. He had been reading the newspaper and saw a job posting for a vice principal at Scappoose Middle School in Scappoose, Oregon. Scappoose is a small town west of Portland by about thirty miles, toward the coast. Steve told me I should go apply, even though I told him that I was not a certified administrator. He kept insisting, so I said I would drive out and talk with them.

When I arrived in Scappoose, I drove to the district office and walked in. I asked the secretary for a copy of the job posting for student management. I also asked her if you needed to be a certified administrator to apply. She told me it was a paid teaching position to carry out the vice-principal's and athletic director's duties. Since it was a teaching position you did not need to have an administrator's license. Just about that time a voice came out of one of the offices and told the secretary to show me in.

When I entered the administrator's office, a man came to the door and introduced himself as Ed, the superintendent of the Scappoose School District. He asked me to sit down and tell him why I came in. After I had a seat, I started telling him why I was there, and that I was looking for a new position. We got along great, and ended up talking for an hour, covering a wide range of topics. After we were done talking, Ed asked if I would return the next day and talk with the middle school principal, Delbert Powell. I told him, "Of course—that would be great," and went on my way.

As I left Scappoose, I drove over to the middle school. Once again, as I sat in my car out front, looking at the middle school building, I thought to myself how great it would be to be at Scappoose Middle. I also thought about how all my experiences, good and bad, had brought me to this opportunity.

When I came back the next day I met with Delbert and Ed. Delbert was a great guy, and I could see his belief in a conservative approach to education. It was just like mine. All three of us educators were on the same wavelength. It was a great discussion, and a great interview. I knew this school was where I belonged. After we were finished, I thanked them for their time and went on my way. I really wanted this job—badly! I tried not to show it. I knew this: they wanted someone who would run a tight ship. With my classroom and coaching experience, I was the guy. I was the best fit; I was perfect for this job!

It only took two hours before the phone rang. Delbert was on the other end of the line. He asked me if I would like to be Scappoose Middle School's new vice-principal. I told him yes, and that I appreciated the opportunity. When I hung up the phone, I could not believe it! I was a new vice-principal. The first thing I did was to call my brother and thank him for his help. He was excited for me and my new position.

When I arrived at Scappoose Middle, Delbert introduced me to the staff, and I learned very quickly that they had worked very hard at getting the school running like a well-oiled machine. The students were respectful, and enjoyed the school atmosphere. It was completely different from Grant High School. I was back in my comfort zone. This school was run with a conservative approach, and it was working. Behavioral problems were small, test scores were up, and the school was clean and well taken care of. My next two years at Scappoose Middle would be the best years in my educational career.

Scappoose Middle was an older school but when Delbert took over, he painted the entire interior and exterior of the school. He had hired teachers that held the line on school expectations. If a student misbehaved, consequences were given. Get this! If a student didn't show up for school or we hadn't heard from the parents, both Delbert and I got in his car, went to their house, knocked on the front door, waited until they got dressed, then brought them back to school. Students didn't skip because they knew we would go find them and bring them back with us.

Farm Boy Go Plow Your Dirt

MY WORST MOMENT AT SCAPPOOSE MIDDLE CAME IN the first week I was there. After school I walked out to the football field and watched the kids practice football. After standing there for a while, this old farmer came up to me and said, "You're the new vice-principal, aren't you?" I turned to him and we introduced ourselves. A few minutes passed, and he asked how I thought the kids were doing. I answered that I thought they were doing pretty well, and having fun. He paused for a moment, and then, in a more serious voice, asked, "How do you *really* think they're doing?" Once again, I kept my answer short, telling him I thought the kids were doing fine. Then I went back to watching.

After a moment, he again pressed me about my answer. By then I'd had just about enough of this guy. I turned to him and said, "You really want to know? The quarterback is handing the ball off to the back wrong. The back doesn't have his hands in the right position to receive the handoff. The lineman's stances are terrible, and the receivers are running bad pass patterns." Then I looked him square in the eye. He looked back at me, commenting, "You're a jerk."

I took a step closer to him, and said, "Listen, farm boy! You don't know a thing about me, so why don't you go sit on your little tractor and plow some dirt!" He didn't like that, so he walked off. I could not believe this guy. Later, I found his son was the coach.

The next day, I was called into the superintendent's office. Ed told me he had received a phone call from "farm boy." Ed wanted to know what had happened. I told him how I tried to be nice, but he just kept pushing and digging at me. Ed said, "Do you know who he was?" I said, "No." Then Ed told me that the "farm boy" was the former superintendent of schools, and he wanted me fired. I was quiet for a moment, and then said, "Ed, you and everyone else really don't know what I can do. Give it some time: get to know me and find out who you hired. If you don't like what you see, then send me on my way." Then Ed said, "You know, Larry, I never did like that guy. And you know what else? He's a jerk, and everyone knows it."

Little did I know that at the end of my first year at Scappoose Middle School, I would receive a thank you letter from the entire school board, thanking me for the fine job I had done. As time went on that first year, I grew to know the staff and students. I realized that even though the school was doing well, something was missing. One morning, I walked into the gym, where students were gathered before school would start. I found them standing around waiting for the bell to ring. I decided to talk with Delbert about providing some activities for the students to enjoy before school and during lunch. He liked the idea and provided me with money to buy a couple of ping-pong and foosball tables along with air hockey. I also grabbed one basketball that could be used for challenge games on the main floor of the gym.

In two weeks, the activities that I had created were in full swing. At the next teacher's meeting I got a round of applause from the staff. They had started to see my direction and how I cared for the students. The kids were having a good time with the new activities and enjoying their free time.

Again, I went to Delbert, and said, "At lunch, when the students are outside on a nice day, they have nowhere to sit and talk when they are done eating in the cafeteria." My idea was to set up gathering stations so students could relax during lunch. Delbert once again thought it might be worth trying. We ordered some picnic tables and set them up on the grass outside the cafeteria. The students started to use them immediately.

The last area I thought needed energy was the school-wide assembly. We asked our students to study hard and behave in the classroom, and I thought it was important to reward those who completed their schoolwork and showed good citizenship in school.

At the start of every sports season I would put on a spirit assembly. I would introduce and honor our sports teams. I would also try to provide humor and excitement for the students. The assemblies were on Fridays, at the end of the school day. I wanted to send the kids home for the weekend with a smile on their faces.

The assemblies were a great way to promote school spirit, and could feature everything from teachers playing in the teacher's band to sumo wrestling to getting a pie in the face. Students had a chance to show off their talents, and a chance to perform in front of their peers.

At the end of every assembly, students would compete for the Spirit Stick. It was a stick about three feet long, painted with the school's colors. I would lead the students from each class in this simple cheer: "We've got spirit, yes we do. We've got spirit, how about you?" I made a big deal over this. A teacher would stand with a sound meter and take a reading so that it was fair. The loudest class won the Spirit Stick until the next assembly. The Spirit Stick was placed in the trophy case in the main hall for students to see as they walked by. A sign indicated who had won it last. It was there for all to see!

Look Out: Ready or Not, Here Comes Santa!

THE FUNNIEST MOMENT I CAN RECALL AT SCAPPOOSE was during the Christmas Vacation Spirit Assembly. We had Delbert, the principal, dressed as Santa Claus, hidden in the closet at the top of the gym's bleachers. During the assembly, when the song "Here Comes Santa Claus" was played, his job was to come down from the closet, waving and saying, "Ho, ho, ho! Merry Christmas, everyone!" There was also a teacher placed at the door of the closet, ready to open it when it was time for Santa to come down the stairs.

But while Santa was in the closet, he got real hot. He decided to take the Santa suit off to cool down, until it was time for his entrance.

Somehow, the timing of the assembly went south. All of a sudden, "Here Comes Santa Claus" came over the loudspeakers. A teacher jumped up and swung the door open, and there sat Santa—the principal of our school—in his underwear.

The students erupted with laughter. Santa quickly grabbed the door handle and slammed the closet door shut. The music stopped, but the kids couldn't stop laughing. Then, once again, the door flew open, and there was a mighty, "Ho, ho, ho—Merry Christmas, everyone!" The song came back on, and Santa came down the stairs, handing out candy. When he got down to the gym floor, he turned and waved, and let out another, "Ho, ho, ho—Merry Christmas, everyone!" Then he left the assembly.

The assembly continued in great fun and laughter. When it was over, the students left school for their Christmas vacation with smiles on their faces. Mission accomplished!

11

RUNNING THE SCHOOLS

Leadership 2000

MY SECOND YEAR AT SCAPPOOSE WENT well, and I decided to apply to Portland State University to become a certified school administrator. I applied and was accepted into the Leadership 2000 program at PSU. It was a year-long commitment during which you studied different areas of education and took a state test. It was forty-five additional college credits. It wasn't easy to do my job at Scappoose Middle and carry a full load at PSU. I already had my master's degree in education, so this was like getting a doctorate.

I did okay, passing the state test and becoming a legal certified public school administrator. I'm writing this because it was not easy for the "little fat boy" to stand up in front of other, very good teachers, and show them my weaknesses. I was once again scared, thinking I wasn't good enough. It seemed that people in education were nice people, but hell-bent on making education or learning complicated, and screwing it up. I would always try to remember the golden rule: *keep it simple, stupid.*

After acquiring my certification, I thought it would be a good idea to apply for the principal's position at Scappoose Middle School, since Delbert would be retiring. I applied, but they gave the position to someone else in the district. Since Delbert had hired me, I thought it might be time to move on. It was kind of sad, because we were all doing so well. I found a classified job posting for a vice principal position in the Springfield School District. I called and took my resume over to downtown Portland's Hilton Hotel, where the interviews were being held. Later that day, I received an interview. The interview went well, and I was offered a position at Hamlin Middle School, in Springfield, Oregon. Since I was now a certified administrator, the pay increase was substantial. I accepted, and I was on my way to another new adventure.

Hamlin Middle School
(1996–2000)

When I arrived at Hamlin Middle School, I was greeted by my new principal, Roger. Roger had been on vacation, and was not a part of my hiring process. He let me know right away that he was unhappy that he wasn't included in my hiring. I didn't let it get me down. Later I found Roger to be very intelligent—and yet one of the laziest guys I had ever run into. Maybe that's why they hired me. They had heard what a hard worker I was.

Hamlin Middle School was 105 miles from Portland, in Springfield, Oregon. Springfield was just across the I-5 freeway from Eugene, Oregon, and located on the banks of the Willamette River. Springfield was somewhat more conservative than Eugene, and it's population had a much lower income. The students came from hard-working families that didn't have a lot of extra money. Hamlin was a large middle school of about a thousand students, and had its share of behavioral problems. Being a conservative educator, I had my work cut out for me.

I could tell, during the first two weeks of school, that Hamlin lacked school spirit and discipline. The first day I walked down the hall, I saw a student take a swing at another student, hitting the teacher who was trying to break it up. To say the least, it was a tough school. It was going to take a conservative approach and some tough love to straighten it out. When I stepped into my office, I did some research, and learned that 7500 students had been sent to the office the year prior. My eyes opened wide—I couldn't believe it. I did some quick math. If this trend continued, I was going to see between forty and forty-five students a day for bad behavior. After seeing this huge number, I went next door and asked Roger why so many students were on referrals. He looked at me, seeming unsurprised by the number. It was jumping out at me that students didn't think it was a big deal to get in trouble. The consequences for student behavior were too light. I knew then, why I was there!

At the first faculty meeting I stood before the teachers and explained my position. I told them that 7500 referrals to the office was unacceptable. I then indicated that the number was going to be cut in half that year. I also let them know that they were paid to teach, and part of their job was to take care of small behavioral problems. My job was to handle the big stuff. I went on to say, "Don't send the small stuff, or I'll send it back. Use your classroom discipline program to handle it. If you don't have one, then meet in your departments and develop one. I'll help you any way I can. Then, if there's a serious problem, send the student to the office, and I will handle it."

It was apparent that the teachers were a little upset. But I stood my ground once again, saying, "No small behavioral referrals."

In the next few months, I used a three-strike system. The first time a student was sent to the office, I issued a small consequence, and explained the new system. The second time, I was more serious. The nice guy was gone, and I would give them an In-School Suspension and call the parent, or issue a Saturday School. The third time, the parents had to come in and conference with me, then take the student home for a three-day suspension. If the student saw me a fourth time, it was a ten-day suspension, parent conference, and warning for possible expulsion and placement on probation.

When a few students got to step three, the word got out. You don't want to see Geigle. Students knew they were going home, and that parents had to leave work, come to the school, and pick them up. The student who I had watched hit a teacher went to step four very quickly, and found himself kicked out of school. He never returned to Hamlin. When students saw their friend get expelled for getting into a fight, they knew I meant business.

As I walked the campus at Hamlin, once again I saw the students standing around before school and during lunch, with little to do. I knew that if kids that had free time and nothing to do, they would make their own excitement. I went to Roger, and talked with him about creating some before-school and lunchtime activities. Roger gave me his blessing, and then gave me some money. Once again, I purchased two foosball tables, two ping-pong tables, and one air-hockey table.

Students immediately started using them. They had fun, and it appeared to be relaxing for them. Because the equipment was used so much, I became a master at repairing the tables. The students knew I was watching for mistreatment of the equipment, so that wasn't a problem.

My next conversation with Roger was about school spirit. I wanted to implement my Spirit Assemblies, introduce the sports teams and create some energy and fun for the students. I also wanted to introduce the mighty "Spirit Stick." The look on his face told me he was a little skeptical, thinking it wouldn't do much. But even though he was not a believer, he was willing to give this new direction a try.

When I planned the first assembly, I asked the teachers to participate. The male teachers put together their own little band, and the female teachers did a fantastic chorus-line, all dressed up in silly costumes. When the kids came away from the first assembly, they were more than excited. They had smiles on their faces, ready to enjoy the whole weekend ahead of them. But I think the teachers were more excited than the students. The process of creating school spirit was in full swing; students were responding to what was happening in a positive way. They knew I was trying to make their school enjoyable and a safe place to learn. At the next week's teacher's meeting, I received a standing ovation. They were starting to see my vision and feel the spirit. Roger also brought me into his office and complemented me on the positive change in school atmosphere.

I wanted to make one more change to let students know we appreciated their good behavior, and how they were getting their work turned in and having good attendance. For their efforts, at the end of every nine weeks I would take at least five busloads of students roller-skating, swimming, or to a movie. It was my way of thanking them for their hard work. Also, now that the assemblies were going well, I told students that if they had a recent referral to the office, or bad attendance, or missed assignments, they would attend a study hall instead of the spirit assembly.

Thurston Shooting
(MAY 21, 1998)

ONE DAY LATE IN MAY 1998, I WAS SITTING IN MY office. Toni, my secretary, came in and told me a student at Thurston High School had a gun and was shooting other students. I couldn't believe what I heard! I went to Roger's office. He was staring out his window, and wouldn't respond to me. His two sons were at Thurston, with the shooter. I told Toni to give the alarm for lockdown. As I spoke, cars came up the school driveway to pick up their kids. They weren't waiting to be told what to do—they just headed straight for the classroom, grabbed their kid, and left. They were parking everywhere—going over curbs and other obstacles to get to their child.

As more news about the shooting came out, students and teachers were jolted. Some were in shock—their children or siblings were in the high school, and possibly dead or wounded. We learned later that Kip Kinkel had shot a number of students, and most were in serious condition or dead.

I think that because I didn't have a loved one at Thurston, I was able to function and secure our building. When the shooting was over and police had secured Thurston High School, classes in the school district were suspended for the rest of the week. We all needed time to recover and evaluate what had happened and what was needed to restart all the schools. Later, we learned that Kip had shot his parents also. To this day, he sits in prison. Hopefully will stay there for the rest of his life for the suffering he caused. It was a sad time. I have never been able to figure out why it happened.

I stayed at Hamlin for four years, working hard every day, even weekends. I felt we were doing a pretty good job until one day when I was talking to the principal, and he indicated that the district office was looking for a new personnel director. Because of Roger's relationship with people all over the district, I told him I thought he was the best choice for the job. Two weeks later, he was named the new personnel director. Roger was leaving, and our new principal was the guy who thought 7500 referrals to the office was a good thing.

From the time Steve walked in the door, the school atmosphere started to go downhill. He was a stickler for the rules, but had no clue about student atmosphere. Now that I look back, I think he was a lousy boss. He didn't like the activities or the assemblies. I knew very quickly that my days at Hamlin were numbered. He tried hard to make me feel bad about my work—he even came in and yelled at me in my office. It was time for me to look for a new school.

But before I left I was surprised to learn that Steve was being transferred back to his old school, and we were getting another principal. I thought there might be hope yet! My optimism was short-lived, though—things went downhill even more. The new principal seemed to dislike me, and I know I disliked her, the instant we were introduced. She was a very liberal idealist, and I was a very conservative thinker. Our philosophies clashed. I felt like she tried to make me, once again, feel bad about my work. My conservative approach was too simple for her. It seemed as if she was bothered that I was so well-liked, and students were drawn to me. Looking back now, it was obvious that she didn't like my having control of the school. It was as though she felt threatened somehow.

She said I could no longer suspend students for bad behavior. She indicated she was not that excited about the activities program. It was as if she was blatantly refusing to give it significance. I think because of our obvious differences in approach, she was hell-bent on destroying my position at Hamlin. I guess she thought that if a student wasn't in school they weren't learning anything. I know some people feel that way, and it might sound good, but my belief is that students need rules, boundaries, and real consequences that mean something. If they can't or won't go by the rules and behave in school, they need to go home and think about it.

After a few months under the new principal, I was done, and ready to move on. Springfield School District was a not a good place for me anymore. At the end of the year I resigned my position and headed back home to Beaverton.

12

OTHER JOBS

The Jenkins Estate
(SUMMER 2000)

I GOT A JOB AT THE JENKINS ESTATE, IN THE SUM-
mer of 2000, after I left Hamlin Middle School. I needed a job—and
I needed it yesterday, if you know what I mean! When I left Hamlin,
I asked for two weeks' pay and the right to leave on the last day of
school. Roger the new personnel director agreed to release me, but
forgot to tell my principal. A few days after leaving, I received a
phone call from the principal. She told me to come back and help
with scheduling for the next school year. I refused, and hung up on
her. She deserved nothing from me; I had moved on.

A week before I left Hamlin, I had applied at the Tualatin Hills
Parks and Recreation Department. They were glad to see me back,
and it was good to be there. My new job was at the Jenkins Estate, as

a supervisor for weddings and other events. The Jenkins Estate was a large, beautiful piece of property in Beaverton. It had been donated to the Tualatin Hills Park and Recreation. The property was full of old-growth fir trees, and large areas consisting of gardens and lawn. Right in the middle stood the rustic lodge that Doctor Jenkins and his wife had lived in for many years. It was filled with beautiful hardwood floors, two large stone fireplaces, and large old-style windows that looked out over the beautifully kept grounds. Coming up to the Jenkins Estate from Farmington Road, the driveway winds through the beautiful trees and gardens and up alongside the old, majestic lodge—with its covered porch that runs the entire length of the house.

The good news about this position was that Linda, my old boss from Cedar Hills Recreation, was my supervisor. When I went in for the interview, we had a short discussion, and I landed the job the next day. The bad news was that it paid nothing compared to my assistant-principal position at Hamlin Middle School.

All summer long I watched weddings take place—mostly on weekends. During the week, people would come up to the estate to preview the property for their event. I would show them the different locations where their event could take place. If they liked one of the locations, they would leave a small deposit and book their event in advance. We had quite a waiting list.

On the weekends before the events would start, the caterers would show up. My job was to show them around the large kitchen to prepare the food. I always tried to kid with them, even though they were pretty busy. I would say that I was the official food tester, and I needed to sample all the food. It worked! Every wedding I would get a free meal and a large piece of wedding cake. I would be sitting in my office and all of a sudden the door would fly open, and all the caterers would enter with a big plate of food, and thank me for my help. I met some pretty nice people, and it turned out to be a very nice summer.

I enjoyed the wonderful old lodge, and thought it was majestic. As time went on, the hot summer nights grew cooler. Fall was just around the corner. I started searching the newspaper for a new teaching position. I knew I would be starting all over again, but I was used to it!

One day I came across an ad in the paper. It read: "PE and Health teacher wanted at Eddyville School, in Lincoln County, Oregon." Once again, like old times, I jumped in my car and drove over to Eddyville. It was a little hitch in the road thirty miles west of Corvallis. If you blinked going through, you might miss it. It was new territory for me—I found myself driving on a road I had never been down before.

When I drove up to the school, I saw an old building that looked like it had been added onto many times. The school was back off the highway about a hundred yards. Even though the building was old, it had a fresh coat of paint, and the lawn surrounding it was freshly cut and well-maintained. I drove up and got out of my car. As I entered the school, I could see that even though it was old, it was clean, and everything looked to be in its proper place.

I went up to the counter and asked the secretary for the application. Since I had brought all my paperwork with me, I sat down at a small table and filled out the forms. I had no problem filling out the answers on the application, and felt confident from years of experience. When I was done, I turned it in and thanked the secretary. She thanked me for applying and said they would let me know.

As I was driving home, I thought about how small the school was. I had figured out from the pictures posted on the bulletin board that there were only eight seniors. If my guess was right, there were only twenty-five students in the whole high school. This would be completely different from anything I had ever done.

The next day, the phone rang, and I was asked to come in for an interview. When I arrived, the secretary showed me to an office at the back of the school. The principal introduced himself as Don Adams. He was about my age—a little taller than me, and a bit overweight. He told me what they were looking for—a little about the history of the school and the students in it. I could tell, once again, that this was a principal with a conservative approach. We talked for a while. He thanked me and said he would let me know in a day or so. I left, once again feeling good about the interview. I had told him about my experience at Hamlin Middle School, and that I was starting over.

As I waited for a call, I wondered if this new teaching position would be enough. The next day, the phone rang. I was offered the job, and accepted. I was on my way to Eddyville, Oregon. It was hard to say goodbye, once again, to the Jenkins Estate. I had been treated so well. Linda, my boss, was wonderful, and I thanked her for helping me.

Eddyville
Charter School

GRADUATION JUNE
FIRST FRIDAY
MID SCHOOL AWARDS

Home Of The
Eagles

School
THE HOME OF THE EAGLES

CHAPTER THIRTEEN

SMALL SCHOOLS

Eddyville K–12
(2001)

EDDYVILLE WAS A NEW EXPERIENCE—different from anything I had done up to that time. No more big classes, and no more exciting football games. The school was so small it was hard to create any excitement. The students were low-key and not much fun. My high school PE class had six students. What do you do with just six kids in PE? As I write this, I wonder how I ever made it through such a boring year. I really have nothing to say about Eddyville; good or bad. It was just too small. If you like small, be my guest. I also had seventh and eighth grade PE. It was a little bigger, but filled with little "jerks" who wanted to cause trouble every day.

One day we were having some free time, during which students picked their own activity. Some kids played basketball, others badminton or wallball. When I explained free time to the students, I told them that if a stray basketball came their way, not to pick it up and throw it. "You might hit someone," I said. It wasn't five minutes later that one of the "jerks" picked up a basketball, threw it the full length of the gym, and hit a little girl in the head. I was so mad and tired of this idiot that I picked up a ball, ran at him, and threw the ball as hard as I could in his direction, hitting the wall next to him with a loud *boom!* It scared him to death. Then I went to see how the little girl was. I thought it was a good lesson for this guy, but I'm sure there are parents reading this who think I acted inappropriately. Maybe I did, but the little "jerk" deserved it.

Later that day, sure enough, in came the parents, wanting the teacher's head for scaring their poor little child. Of course they had no thoughts about their child hurting the little girl with a possible concussion. When I met with the principal, the parents and student were there. I told the parents my story—how I had *just* told the kids not to pick up the basketballs and throw them because someone might get hit. You could see that the parents didn't want to talk about that—they just wanted to focus on what I had done. I told the parents that I was sorry for throwing the ball against the wall, but I was upset about the little girl getting hurt.

Don, the principal, looked at the parents and said, "If your son would have followed the classroom rules, none of this would have happened. Take your son home for the rest of the day. Tomorrow he's suspended. Mr. Geigle, you may return to class." I couldn't believe it—that was it! A student had done something wrong and got a serious consequence for his actions. The principal had backed up his teacher! I never had another problem with that student for the rest of the year. At the end of the year, his father came up to me and told me that I was his son's favorite teacher.

As time went on, students started responding to my efforts to create school spirit, and once again the atmosphere of the school improved. Late into the school year I was told that they wanted me to be the new Athletic Director. I was also going to be the new head football and baseball coach. But that didn't last long.

One day, Don, the principal, called an emergency teacher's meeting after school. Don informed us that Eddyville was going to be closed down because of budget cuts. He told us that teachers would be transferred to a new assignment. Since I was so new, I figured, they wouldn't reassign me. Time to look for a new teaching position.

When the year was over, we said our goodbyes. I thought I was done in Lincoln County Schools. I headed back to Beaverton and started enjoying the summer. Four weeks later, I called Don at Eddyville School, and to my surprise, found that I had been transferred to Siletz School on the Siletz Indian Reservation. I guess I still had a job.

I started thinking about how tough teaching was getting, and how trying to deal with my trauma issues might be more stressful than trying to find something else. Students weren't behaving, and parents backed neither teachers nor most administrators. I wondered what the next year was going to bring, and asked myself if I could teach effectively. I knew my conservative approach to education was being dismantled by too many liberal, expensive, complicated programs.

On to Siletz School
(2002)

SILETZ WAS TUCKED AWAY IN THE COASTAL MOUN-tains of the Siletz Indian Reservation. Newport, Oregon was just twenty miles west. This was another school filled with liberal ideas and low test scores. There was a constant lack of discipline, and students felt free to act out. I was out of my comfort zone.

One of my first encounters was with a student named Eddie. He was a Native American kid and thought he owned the school. He would harass and bully the other students. He was big and strong, so the other kids stayed out of his way. I found that if you didn't confront this kid for pushing others around he was okay—but the minute you stopped him, he was in your face, big time.

About the third day of school I let Eddie know that bullying other kids was not going to happen in my classroom—I told him to stop. Underneath the tough exterior, I really think there was a pretty good kid, but someone needed to confront him and teach him how to respect others.

A few weeks into the school year I was in the gym playing basketball with some of the students and saw Eddie grab another student from the sidelines. He wanted to play against me and another student and show us who was boss. He told me to pick a partner, and we would play to eleven. I agreed, and found another kid and was ready to play. When the game started, Eddie got the basketball, and right off the bat drove (or should I say "bullied") his way to the basket, and made a lay-up for two points. I then took the ball out and passed it to my partner; he passed it back and I shot a three-point basket. We were ahead three to two. Once again, Eddie got the ball, didn't pass, and drove straight for the basket. I then stepped directly in his path and didn't move. Eddie ran into a brick wall, and for the first time in his life he couldn't bully his way out. He got real upset and even acted like he was going to hit me. I stood my ground and the tears started to run down Eddie's face. The game was over.

I thought for sure he was going to run to his parents, but he didn't. As time went on, Eddie got the idea that I was not afraid of him. When he was respectful towards others, I complimented him. When he was disrespectful, I sat him down and wouldn't let him participate. Sometimes he walked out of class and I would mark him a skip. After many months, Eddie started to catch on. I even think he liked me. The PE classes were fun, and he wanted to be a part of the action.

We didn't know it at the time, but Eddie and I would meet again twelve years later. When he saw me, his face lit up, and we talked for a while. I realized he had turned into a pretty nice young man. He was working as a security guard at the Chinook Winds Casino, in Lincoln City. I also realized how big he had gotten—I thought to myself that I wouldn't want to mess with him now.

Every day, I saw the teachers at Siletz working hard to give their students a good education. But the approach they were using was weak, and the students took advantage of it. They weren't given real consequences for their bad behavior.

I did not really enjoy Siletz. There was no real school atmosphere or spirit, and the students misbehaved a lot. I called the district office later, and asked them to look at my resume and think about sending me to one of the high schools at the end of the year. The two years at Eddyville and then Siletz were getting me down!

Then one day in health class the students were busy studying. One of the students started talking and distracting others trying to do their school work. I told him to quiet down and get to work. He gave me that *I-don't-need-to-listen-to-you* look. A few minutes later, I told him again not to disturb others. He looked at me and told me he didn't need to be quiet. I told him to pick his books up and go down to the office. With a look of disrespect he said, "No!" I told him to go to the office. He again refused, so I walked over, grabbed him by his collar, and literally dragged him out of the classroom and up to the office. I sat him down, returned to the classroom, and continued to teach. Two minutes later, the principal was at my door. He said, "Mr. Geigle, come with me please. Another teacher will watch your class for you."

After we walked down to the office, I told the principal what had happened. He said, "I'm sending you home for the rest of the day."

I couldn't believe it! I told him that if he sent me home, the student would think he could do it again, and that would send the wrong message. He sent me home, anyway, so I could calm down.

I thought he was a weak administrator. The student should have received a talking to and a real consequence for acting out. I should have called the office for help, and waited for someone to come down and escort the student back to the office. I admit I should have done that differently, but teachers make mistakes, and students shouldn't feel like they can get teachers in trouble.

The parents came in and were not happy with the way I had grabbed their son. I apologized for grabbing him. I also told them I regretted not calling the office for help. The parents seemed to calm down after talking. My principal told me in front of the parents that next time I should follow procedure and call for help. The student acting out in class never received a consequence. We had lost ground once again, and the student won.

My relationship with that particular student changed; I think because he saw that in the classroom it was my way or the highway. He did not test me again. Because I had put the brakes on his behavior, he knew that if he did act out, I would call the office and he would be gone.

I would like to explain my thoughts about setting the line in a classroom and not being backed up by the principal. I'm talking to you as a football coach and teacher now. When a football game is played, it's important for your team to set the tone. I tell my offensive linemen they must block the opposing linemen backwards down the field, or we will lose. I tell our running backs that they must make yardage running the ball or we lose. In other words, we need to show the other team we mean business, or we won't be respected. On defense, I preach to my players that our defensive line can't be pushed around—if they are, we will lose. I also tell them that our team needs to do a good job tackling the ball carrier. Finally, we need to make one or two great hits. I mean knock the whoop-tee-do out of the other team.

I know it might sound bad, but even if it draws a penalty, it's worth it, because it sets a tone. Sometimes pitchers will throw at a batter in a baseball game, just to set the tone. My point is simply this: Sometimes a teacher in a classroom must set the tone, too. It may not be pretty, and it may seem a little rough on one of the students. But it's vital for the success of the class and all the students. *Remember: I'm the teacher, coach, or parent. I set the tone—not the kid!*

After the end of the year at Siletz, I submitted a request to transfer to a high school, and it was accepted. I was going to be the new PE and Health teacher at Taft High School, in Lincoln City. I said goodbye to Siletz School, and was excited to be teaching back in a high school setting.

Chapter Fourteen

TEACHING AND COACHING ON THE COAST

Paula Christine Anet Nortness Geigle, My New Wife
(2002)

IT HAD BEEN THIRTEEN YEARS SINCE I WAS MARried to Debbie and had my two beautiful girls. I haven't talked much about my girls, because quite frankly they weren't in my life for a lot of those thirteen years. Somewhere along the line, I began to feel left out of their lives. What their mother—like most people who knew me—didn't realize was that I was fighting a constant battle from my trauma. I was still fighting with what happened so many years before on the *USS Mars*. My relationships with other women were a constant reminder of my lack of trust. Every relationship would end the same. I would try again and again to feel secure and safe about caring for someone, and it just didn't happen.

One day I went to get a haircut in Newport, Oregon. When I sat down in the chair, an attractive stylist asked me how I would like my hair cut. I told her I would like a light trim. As she cut my hair, I noticed some very nice features about this woman, and I was drawn to her. She had pretty eyes, a great laugh, and a gorgeous smile. I would later realize that with the apron off, she was a beautiful woman. She had a movie star figure. I thought, *Wow!* At one point while I was making small talk and she was snipping away, she stopped and asked, "Are you flirting with me?" I said, "Yes, I am!" She laughed, but ignored my answer. When she was done, I went to the counter to pay. I found a piece of paper and wrote down my phone number. I didn't hear from her, so I decided to contact her. A few days later, we talked on the phone, and decided to see a movie. That was the beginning of our relationship. Even though it hasn't been perfect, we've stood by each other through good and bad, ever since that first date.

At that time, I had just been transferred to Siletz School. I had bought a motor home, and had parked it down in Newport so my commute to Siletz School would be reduced. I had rented out my condominium in Portland; also the one in Eugene. Neither condo was close enough for my work. After Christy and I dated for a while, I liked being with her so much, I started staying at her place.

Several months later, we jumped in my car and headed down to Reno to get married. I thought to myself, *That girl has a fierce temper, but the kindest heart I've ever seen.* I decided to give it a try. I always tell people we got married in the house of Elvis, but it was really just a small chapel. It only took a few minutes. Once we were married, we walked outside, got back in the car, and headed home as husband and wife. (Boy, was she lucky!) On the way home, we spent a night at Salishan Resort, in Lincoln City. To my surprise, as we were having dinner, Christy walked over to the piano. Before I knew it, she was singing Barbra Streisand songs. We had fun that night and the next morning we headed on home to a new life together.

Taft High School
(2003–2005)

WHEN I HEARD I HAD BEEN TRANSFERRED TO TAFT High School in Lincoln City. I got real excited. I was back in a larger high school again after leaving Grant eight years before. I got in my car and headed over to Taft to see what it looked like. I went right to the gym, and as I was standing there looking things over, a secretary came in and asked if she could help me. I introduced myself and informed her that I was the new PE teacher for the upcoming school year. She said, "Congratulations, and welcome." I later became very good friends with her, and found her to be a special part of the school.

I went in the office to say hello to Dave, the principal. He gave me a warm welcome, and we had a great conversation. As we talked, I learned more about the school and its' needs. I then asked Dave if there were any coaching assignments available. I told him a little about my coaching experience, and asked to be considered for football and baseball.

A few days later, after talking with Dave, I received a call. It was Jack, the varsity football coach. We talked for a while about my experience and where I had coached. He seemed to be a great guy. At the end of our conversation he wanted to know if I was interested in helping the varsity running backs along with being the defensive coordinator for the JV football team. I went ahead and accepted those positions; I was coaching football again, and excited to get started.

During that summer, I got to know Ken, who was the varsity defensive coordinator. Both Jack (the head coach) and Ken were good guys, and great to work with. The more I got to know the principal and other staff, the more I felt back in my comfort zone. Once again, I was having fun.

In football that year, the varsity lost a few, but we knew the next year we would be great. The JV team went undefeated; they were aggressive and fast. It wasn't hard to set the right tone on the field and earn the respect of other teams in the league. I developed some great relationships during the year, and earned the respect of staff members.

Paul, our varsity line coach and JV offensive coordinator, was a very smart guy. He was too smart for his own good, and it hurt his coaching. Instead of ten plays, Paul wanted to call forty plays. I think football wasn't complicated enough for him. After one of the games, when the offense hadn't done well, I got after him. I told him he was screwing up the team. He was putting too many plays in at practice, and it was confusing the kids. He didn't understand, so we had a little discussion about "keeping it simple, stupid"—an old saying that football coaches use when a coach has complicated the game too much. I thought for sure I had lost his friendship. I was wrong, because after that he settled down and started to listen to me, we became pretty good friends. I liked Paul—he was a great guy.

Coaching Football

SINCE THE START OF MY COACHING CAREER AT Highland Park, I have always remembered that first football season. I talked about how important it was to keep the game simple. A football team needs to run like a fine-tuned machine. To do this, players must not have to think about what they are doing; they must be able to react to the situation on the football field. That's why you run the same offensive plays or defense schemes hundreds of times over and over, so the players become consistent. Run too many plays or too many defenses and you will screw it up. If your football team is doing different drills or plays every day in practice, you will not play effectively in games. Other teams will beat you because you've made too many changes and your players will get confused. That's the beauty of coaching football; creating a beautiful masterpiece of teamwork. Everyone knows what to do, and when and how to do it. *Please remember*—there is absolutely no shortcut to winning or becoming a good football team.

Taft Baseball Goes to the Playoffs

AFTER FOOTBALL WAS OVER AND THE STUDENTS HAD an idea who I was, I would ask them how baseball was going. We talked a lot, and then one day one of the players told me there was going to be a change in baseball. The head coach was stepping down. The students wanted to know if I would coach them. A few days later I was offered the position, but turned it down. I was reluctant because of my trauma issues, and continued to say no. Finally the athletic director came to me. He indicated that he was getting phone calls from parents asking if I would be the new head baseball coach. After giving it careful consideration, I accepted the job.

At the first practice, I got after the players pretty good, and set the tone. My ability in baseball coaching appeared quickly. I worked their tails off. We won our first two games, and then we headed to Southern Oregon and played a tournament in Medford. We never lost a game and brought home the first-place trophy. We went on to win our first sixteen games and were rated number two in the state of Oregon. The team was doing well.

Then the sky opened up and it rained for two weeks. When it was over two of our players were injured. One with a sprained ankle from skateboarding, and the other with a back injury from riding a motorcycle. These players were key to our success, and these setbacks took the wind out of our sails. The energy and focus was gone. We had peaked too early, and I knew it. We went into a slump and lost our first game after the rain stopped. Before we recovered, we had lost to Sherwood High School once, and to Newport High twice. We didn't win the league, but we did head to the state playoffs for the first time in twenty years. The season had been a great success and the kids were happy with their efforts. We ended up losing our first state playoff game 2–1; the season was over. I might add that the team had set a new state record for home runs in a single season: we hit forty-seven over the fence.

Toward the end of baseball, Dave, the principal, called me into his office. When I got there, Mike, the athletic director, was sitting at the meeting table. I had a seat and Dave began explaining that Mike was going to retire at the end of the year. He went on to say that both he and Mike thought I would be a good replacement. Mike then explained how the transition would take place. I would have to attend league athletic meetings the rest of the year. My teaching load would be reduced to half-time so I could learn the job. We talked for a while longer about the transition. When the meeting was over I told them I would let them know the next day.

On my way home, I kept thinking about becoming the new athletic director. I knew I wouldn't be able to coach the next year, but I was already thinking I wanted the job. It provided me with an office, and it would reduce my trauma issues by only having to teach half a day. When I got home, I told Christy. After a short discussion, she thought it would be good for me and good for the school.

Taft High School
(ATHLETIC DIRECTOR, 2005–2007)

WHEN SCHOOL LET OUT FOR THE SUMMER OF 2005, Mike retired and took off for the state of Washington, with big dreams of fishing. He sold his beautiful house, bought a boat, and went sailing off into the wild, blue water! As soon as he left, I wasted no time moving my stuff in, and throwing his stuff into the trash can. I had a completely new idea of how the athletic director's office should look. I wanted people to know when they came through my office door where they were and who I was.

I found the latest school team pictures tucked away in a file cabinet. I took them out, framed them, and hung them on the walls. When athletes came in, they liked seeing their team's pictures while talking with me. I contacted the other athletic directors in the league to let them know I was on board. I double-checked all athletic schedules for the upcoming school year. I sent for my copy of the grade sheets to make sure student athletes were okay to play. I also checked the referee's schedule to make sure we would have officials. I knew there was going to be a lot to do when I took the job. I loved every minute of it. I was so busy I had no time to worry about my problems. The only activities I felt nervous about were wrestling and track. To be honest, those weren't my favorite sports, but I always made sure to put the same importance on each of the sports, to be fair.

I spent many nights at the school, watching over athletic events, making sure everything went smoothly. It was also great to be a part of the hiring process. I wanted Taft to have the best coaches we could find. I also wanted to help remove coaches that were there for the wrong reasons. Yes, we fired a few.

My most intense memory was of a Friday night boys' basketball game. It was windy at the coast that night; the electricity went out, and the lights went off. There were a lot of people on the bleachers in the dark. Lucky for us, we had an emergency backup generator that took over, and the lights came back on. Then we finished the game.

The next two years went by pretty fast. I enjoyed being in education once again.

"Larry! The House Is on Fire!"

WHILE I WAS AT TAFT HIGH SCHOOL, CHRISTY AND I decided to buy a house closer to my job. We looked, finally finding a small two-bedroom house overlooking Devil's Lake, in Lincoln City. We knew right away that it was a great little house. I found out a few days later that it was owned by my Boy Scout leader from back in the 60s. Christy and I both loved it, so we bought it. The inside had a large, old-fashioned wood stove set in the middle of the living room. Vaulted cedar ceilings and wood beams added to the rustic feel. The two bedrooms were good-sized, but the house only had one bathroom, with a tub and shower. Off the dining room were sliding glass doors that led out to a huge deck. We even had a view of the lake off in the distance.

We moved in and went right to work fixing it up. We created more of an open concept in the kitchen, and repainted all the cupboards. When Christy and I go to work on a project, we both have a pretty good eye—so it turned out sweet! After we were there a few years, we both agreed to turn the single-car garage into a family room and art studio for Christy. We also added a shower to the half bathroom I had built earlier. Everything was done in cedar. It smelled really good.

I had just finished the remodel when Christy brought a problem to my attention. The lights seemed to be randomly flickering off and on. It bothered her more than me. She kept after me, saying that something was not right and that it was scaring her. Her parents' house had burned down in the early 80s, so she was pretty sensitive to the threat. I went ahead and hired an electrician to come out and have a look. He found a worn-out part in the breaker box, and replaced it with another used worn-out part. He did that because our breaker box was so old he couldn't find a new part—big mistake! A few days later, the part split, then arced, setting the side of our house on fire. I was in the shower when I heard Christy yelling, "Larry! Larry! The house is on fire!" I jumped out of the shower, completely nude, and yelled, "Call the fire department, now!" I then wrapped myself in a towel and continued to run out the back door to the side of the house. When I got there, I saw the side of the house in flames. I picked up the hose and was about to spray the fire when I remembered that water and electricity don't mix. I put the hose down and ran into the house to put some pants on.

The first firetruck was arriving, so Christy and I went to the front yard to watch our house burn. We were obviously upset about our home and losing all our possessions. It was also Christy's birthday. As we stood watching the house burn, her phone started ringing. Her sister and brothers sang, "Happy birthday to you, happy birthday to you"—as flames shot into the air. To say the least, it was quite a night. We spent the next month and a half at the Chinook Winds Casino Hotel, while they cleaned and repaired our house. I ended up rebuilding the entire family room and office a second time.

The End of My Days at Taft
(2008-2009)

ALL GOOD THINGS MUST COME TO AN END, SOONER or later. At the beginning of the 2008 school year, there was a rumor going around that Taft High School was going to incorporate with the middle school. This would mean that they would close down the separate middle school so that it could become a new grade school. This was happening because the school district had hired a new superintendent, and he wanted the grade school kids out of danger from earthquakes or tsunamis. We knew the coast was going to be hit with a major earthquake, we just didn't know when.

After school started in 2008 the rumor of a combined middle and high school became real. We started having meetings to formulate what that building would look like. Dave, my principal, was under attack by the new superintendent and middle school principal. Taft High state test scores weren't that great, and they were blaming him. Later, he was demoted to vice-principal, and Steve, the middle school principal, was going to be the principal of the new school. This upset me a lot, since Dave was a solid foundation for Taft. He knew all the parents and even the grandparents of most of our students. I knew he was doing a good job, but the superintendent wanted Dave gone. Dave ended up leaving Taft, and became the principal of South Salem High School—one of the largest high schools in the state of Oregon. He continues to do well.

After I met the new principal, I knew once again my days were numbered. Steve was very liberal in his thinking, and he talked a mile a minute. I thought he should be selling refrigerators or hairspray. He was not my cup of tea—it wasn't a good fit.

The new principal—I had named him the "Glad Happy Salesman"—hired a new vice-principal. I've always put the kids first, and I really believed this new vice-principal was not a good choice. As the story goes, this new vice-principal was a high school track coach. One of his track athletes received a cut to his arm and instead of bandaging the cut, he proceeded to treat the cut as though he were a momma cat, tending to her wounded kitten! I couldn't believe it until I went to the computer and looked it up. According to what the computer told me, he had done it more than once. He had been sued and fired from his last teaching position. He took a job with the state department for five years, and was now working his way back in as our new vice-principal. *Really!* I couldn't believe it!

One morning, later in the school year, the new high school principal—the Glad Happy Salesman—came into the athletic office and sat down. He looked at me and said, "Larry, it looks like you don't want to be a part of my team next year." I admitted to being upset and thinking Dave had been a better choice for principal. He didn't like hearing that. I also told him I thought he was a "jaw-flapper and not sincere." I must have been crazy, but I let it out! He looked at me again, and told me I was being transferred to Ocean Lake, one of Lincoln City's elementary schoools, for the next school year. I told him that was fine, and to do what he needed to do. Then he left. Other teachers couldn't believe what I had done. I just knew I couldn't work for the Glad Happy Salesman. In my opinion he was a fake.

The rest of the year, tensions were high. Everyone wondered what the next year would bring. I knew that my trauma issues had, once again, put me in a position to have to start over. I had no idea what was in store for me at Ocean Lake Elementary. The last thing I wanted was to teach elementary PE. Once again, I would be out of my comfort zone. At the end of the school year, I said my goodbyes and never went back. The new athletic director was fired a year later for mishandling a theft from the school. The vice-principal, the Licker, became the athletic director. He only lasted a year—when he was caught stealing money from the athletic fund. The school test scores never got better and the Glad Happy Salesman moved on to retirement.

I want to take a moment before moving on to say that I have met some wonderful people in education. Like everywhere in life, there are always some takers. They will do anything to help themselves get to a more powerful place. My hat goes off to the givers. They are the ones who do the hard work, and ask for nothing in return. They are the true heroes.

Ocean Lake Elementary
(2009-2011)

AT THIS POINT IN MY TEACHING CAREER I WAS PRETTY
tired of all the politics. The real story was that my PTSD, which had
not been diagnosed so many years earlier, had really worn me down.
Back in 1978, I had gone into the veteran's hospital and asked to
have my chin evaluated. The doctors took a five minute look and
told me I was fine. They never asked me how I was doing, nor did
they seem to care. Why didn't they ask if I was having any problems
related to my injury? Back then, they seemed to think that if you
weren't bleeding, you were ok. I didn't want to make a big deal out
of what I was feeling, because like everyone else, I just wanted to be
normal. Sometimes I wonder how my life would have been different
if I hadn't been hit in the face with that cable; or battled that staph
infection; or had an allergic reaction to penicillin; or had so many
panic attacks; or been able to sleep at night and wake up refreshed;
or been able to trust the ones I loved; or been so angry, obsessive,
scared, or controlling.

I showed up at Ocean Lake Elementary the next year, and was
greeted well. I had a small office in the back of the gym—it was more
like a storage room than an office. I won't try to kid anyone, teaching
younger students was not my strength. They were loud, not very well
behaved, and full of the wrong kind of energy. I figured out very
quickly that I needed to have lots of activities that kept the kids moving and involved. Even though this was a tough PE teaching assignment, I did okay, and the students enjoyed my classes. My principal
was as liberal as they come, and the school payed a price for it. It was
a mess every day when I walked out into the halls. Students were
running, fighting, and not really worried about consequences. I tried
to be a good employee, but in my opinion, the principal wasn't doing
the right thing. I went through some tough days that first year.

My approach was always conservative, simple, and to-the-point. Once again, students tried to battle my system and lost. I had twenty-eight years of experience under my belt, and had "been there / done that" many times. After a while, they started to see what I was about, and jumped on board. My PE classes became very popular, and the other teachers commented on how much the students enjoyed them. I had set the tone for a good classroom. Every day the principal stepped out into the hall to slow down kids from running to PE. When they got to class, I didn't do a lot of talking; I got them right into activities. My thought was to get them moving, and to wear them out so they would sit still in their other classes and learn more.

One of my big concerns was the size of the gym. The cement walls were just inches away from the out-of-bounds line painted on the gym floor. If a student didn't stop fast enough, he or she would collide with a cement wall—and the wall always won. I brought it up to Jack, the principal, and he indicated that the gym was due for a remodel very soon. Until that happened, I decided to hang large red mats on the walls for padding. That way, the students got to enjoy a competitive atmosphere. They loved it.

I made it through the first year, but was having trouble thinking about coming back for a second year. It was getting depressing for me, so I came up with an idea. I found a half-time position at Forest Grove High, teaching half-time health. I had gone to my principal and asked that if I could find a half-time PE teacher, would he be willing to let me go half-time at Ocean Lake and half-time at Forest Grove High School. He agreed, so I applied to Forest Grove High School and got the position.

I had already talked with my friend, Jim, about the half-time position. In my book, Jim was another great conservative educator who ran a good classroom. He had the right stuff, and when we coached baseball together he was great. Jack went ahead and hired him half-time. So, every other day, I would travel to Forest Grove and teach health, and Jim would take my PE classes at Ocean Lake Elementary. It worked great, and I made it through the second year. My students at Forest Grove High were some of the best students I had ever had. They showed me respect and kindness every day I was there.

I knew I wouldn't be returning to Ocean Lake, so I started looking for a new athletic director position. I interviewed at Clatskanie High School for a half-time position as athletic director, and got the job. In the interview, I was relaxed and calm. Because of my time and experience, I knew all the right answers. I was hired the next day and on my way to Clatskanie. At the end of the year, I said goodbye to Ocean Lake, and moved on to Clatskanie High.

Clatskanie High: The Last Stop
(2011–2012)

TAKING THE POSITION AT CLATSKANIE MEANT THAT Christy and I would have to rent out our lake house and find a place to live near Clatskanie. We did this, and I went into Clatskanie with great energy, excited to be athletic director in another high school.

Although I gave it my all, there were some practices going on at Clatskanie that I didn't care for. Some of my concerns were based on some very questionable approaches, and, quite frankly, a not very smart policy by the school district. I did my best to change these things, and clean up what I could in the athletic department. Every school district has a little different way of doing things. Clatskanie was no different. It was hard for them to change. I was an "outsider," and from the start, there were good old boys on the school board who couldn't stand the change. I went head-to-head with them and lost. The superintendent was afraid of these people taking his job.

At the end of the year the athletic director's job was given to a new principal, and my position was eliminated.

The principal who hired me at Clatskanie had decided to leave, and found another position in Cresswell, Oregon. During the summer I received a phone call from him. He asked if I would come to Cresswell, Oregon for an interview to be his new half-time athletic director. I went down for the interview and was told the next day that I had the job. When I got home, I told my wife, and we talked for a while. I decided not to take it. I felt that I was done working, and decided to enjoy retirement, and work on trying to increase the compensation percentage rate I received from Veterans Affairs. I have had no regrets about that decision. I knew that PTSD had taken its toll on me, my family, and my career. As you can see, I traveled a long and winding road to survive. I had many stops and starts along the way—some good, some bad. By the way, I read in the newspaper that Clatskanie School District was sued for male students sexually harassing a female student. Doesn't surprise me!

Back to the Beach

WHEN MY TEACHING CAREER ENDED AT CLATSKANIE, we moved back to our little lake house in Lincoln City. Christy was happy to be back at the beach again, and I guess I was too. At the time, my PTSD was being evaluated by Veterans Affairs. I was in a struggle with them about the destruction it had caused me and my career, and how it was the reason I retired. The VA had a hard time believing veterans could be affected by trauma from an event that occurred many years earlier in Vietnam. My wife sent a twenty-page letter outlining what it was like to be married, for ten years, to a person with PTSD. I also acquired letters from co-workers, my brothers, and friends. I traveled to the veterans' hospital to plead my case on a weekly basis. I was bound and determined to get them to see how much PTSD was affecting my everyday life. Finally, I decided to see a trauma expert. When I did, I was tested and evaluated. It was determined that I suffered from serious PTSD. Within a week, the trauma expert had sent a letter to the VA, stating their findings. The VA could not dispute the evaluation, and granted 80 percent compensation back to 2009.

Finally, as I think back to the beginning of my story, when I was that 5 year old child looking down that steep hill in front of our house... I've never once regretted the thrilling ride this life has given me. Even living all these years with PTSD, trial and error has made me the man I am today. Life goes one... and God willing, there will be more hills to fly down... before the road ends.

ACKNOWLEDGMENTS

I want to thank my wife, Paula (Christy) Geigle, for her help in editing this book and for painting the cover illustration of me as a young man.

I wrote this book in an effort to help my children (Kristyn and Heather) and my grandchildren (Logan, Landon, Hailey, and Carter) know and understand their father and grandfather.

I would also like to pay tribute to all the fine educators and coaches who have influenced my classrooms and athletic teams along the way. I enjoyed our many exciting victories as well as our moments of defeat, and how we never quit or gave up.

This book is also an acknowledgment of the three Geigle boys—the sons of Hughbert Leon and Iva June Geigle. We will always remember the great times, and we love you and think of you often.

I would like to thank Linfield College for providing me with the opportunity to play football, and taking the time to truly care about my future.

Lastly, I would like to acknowledge my brothers in the military, who struggle with PTSD and other afflictions as a result from serving their country.

Lightning Source UK Ltd.
Milton Keynes UK
UKHW01f0621241018
331108UK00008B/463/P